**Editor**
Kim Fields

**Editorial Project Manager**
Mara Ellen Guckian

**Editor-in-Chief**
Sharon Coan, M.S. Ed.

**Illustrators**
Kevin Barnes
Kelly McMahon

**Cover Artist**
Brenda DiAntonis

**Art Manager**
Kevin Barnes

**Art Director**
CJae Froshay

**Imaging**
James Edward Grace
Rosa C. See

**Product Manager**
Phil Garcia

**Publishers**
Rachelle Cracchiolo, M.S. Ed.
Mary Dupuy Smith, M.S. Ed.

**Full Color**

# Literacy Centers & Nursery Rhymes

## Volume 1

Pre K–1

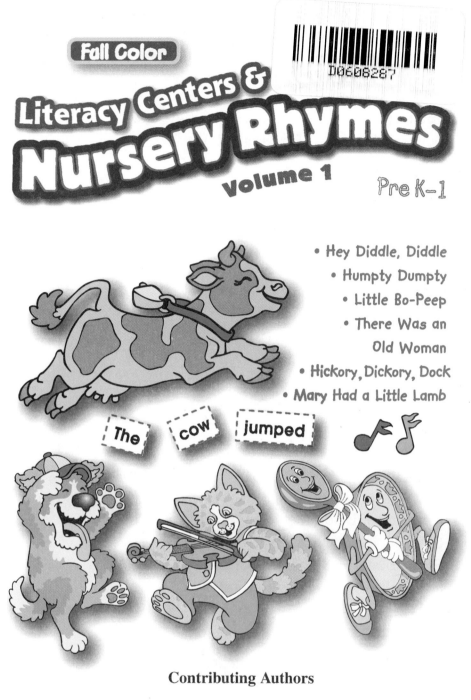

- Hey Diddle, Diddle
- Humpty Dumpty
- Little Bo-Peep
- There Was an Old Woman
- Hickory, Dickory, Dock
- Mary Had a Little Lamb

The cow jumped

**Contributing Authors**

*Bobbie Wilson, Karen Brown,
Mara Guckian, Dede Dodds, M.S. Ed.*

***Teacher Created Materials, Inc.***
6421 Industry Way
Westminster, CA 92683
www.teachercreated.com

**ISBN-0-7439-3396-6**

*©2004 Teacher Created Materials, Inc.*

Made in U.S.A.

# Table of Contents

# Table of Contents (cont.)

# Introduction

Nursery rhymes are short, rhyming poems that have been delighting young children for centuries. The original rhymes, also known as jingles, songs, or ditties, date back to the 18th century. Rhymes are a form of classic literature easy for the young to appreciate. Each rhyme tells a story, most often with an unusual, if not implausible, plot.

Nursery rhymes are a wonderful way to promote a variety of literacy skills including oral language development, phonemic awareness, phonics, fluency, comprehension, and vocabulary. But literacy skills are just the beginning! Coloring, cutting, and assembling the mini books and stick puppets will offer opportunities to improve fine motor skills. Children will also develop self-esteem as they perfect their recitation of each rhyme. Young children take great pride in being able to recite entire rhymes by themselves. Creatively, children benefit as well. Exposure to rhyming words encourages children to make up their own rhymes. They sing rhymes, retell them, and act them out. Older children can write or dictate stories, make puppets, and draw pictures about the rhymes.

*Literacy Centers & Activities for Nursery Rhymes, Volumes 1 & 2,* offer a variety of activities to use when sharing rhymes with students. There is no one right way to use the materials in this book. Some materials, such as the action folders and the sentence strips, are geared initially toward whole-group activities. Later, they can be recopied and used individually by students for reinforcement activities. The craft stick puppets and mini books can be prepared as a whole class, at centers, or individually. Once completed, the finished items can be shared one on one, in small groups, or during center time. Later, the puppets and mini books can be shared with family members at home. Below is an overview of the materials offered for each rhyme.

## Nursery Rhyme Mini Posters

Each colorfully illustrated nursery rhyme mini poster comes ready to laminate and display in the classroom. Copies can be made so that each child can read along, point to spaces between words, note punctuation, etc.

## Action Folders

These unique visual aids were designed to introduce the rhymes and should enchant young students. The full-color patterns are sure to make these folders classroom keepsakes.

## Mini Books

Four- or six-page, easy-to-assemble mini books are included for each rhyme. Students may color the illustrations to make the books truly their own, and read the books to others.

## Sentence Strips/Picture Cards

The sentence strips were constructed in large print with exaggerated spacing, using a child-friendly font. They can be cut and laminated for use in pocket charts during whole class-or small-group instruction. Full-color picture cards accompany each set of strips.

## Stick Puppet Patterns

The puppet patterns were designed to be cut out, colored by children, and attached to craft sticks. They can be used to retell the nursery rhymes or to create new adventures for the characters. An additional set of full-color patterns is included for use in a center or during teacher reenactments.

# Why Teach Nursery Rhymes?

The sing-song nature of nursery rhymes enables most children to learn them easily. Once learned, children enjoy repeating them over and over again. Nursery rhymes can be used to develop or improve a variety of literacy skills including the following:

**Oral Language**—One of the hallmarks of a child whose oral language is advancing is that he or she can tell a story over time (and then . . . and then . . . and then . . . ). It is important for children to be given time to finish a story in sequence, in their own words, and not to be asked to "hurry up and finish" or "tell us later." Nursery rhymes are perfect stories to retell in sequence. And, since they are short, they can be memorized relatively quickly.

**Phonemic Awareness**—A child is said to be "phonemically aware" when he or she can identify individual sounds (phonemes) in oral language. The nature of nursery rhymes encourages children to develop phonemic awareness by focusing on rhyming word endings (rimes) and extending word play. Activities also focus on awareness of beginning sounds (onsets). The activities provide opportunities for beginning readers to enhance their ability to hear and discriminate sounds. The letters that appear in question marks should be voiced as sounds not as letter names.

**Phonics**—Phonics refers to the association of letters (graphemes) with the sounds (phonemes) they represent. This sound/letter relationship is essential for decoding. A key strategy is to group words with similar patterns or rimes (phonograms). In word families, such as *fall, ball, wall,* or *spoon, moon, noon,* each word contains the same pattern (chunk). Once the pattern is internalized, readers can generalize to other words with similar rimes.

**Vocabulary Development**—Reading and sounding out new words are much easier for children who are already familiar with the words. The unusual words included in many of the rhymes enable children to add new vocabulary to their repertoire. Discussion about the rhymes can also increase vocabulary skills. Matching word cards to picture cards, and text to illustrations, also enhances vocabulary development.

**Fluency**—Fluency is an important and frequently undervalued component of reading. Fluency is the ability to read accurately and quickly with minimal errors. Oral fluency is marked by intonation (expression). Reciting nursery rhymes is a wonderful way to practice this skill at a very young age. Oral reading using the sentence strips, mini books, and mini posters extends the opportunities to improve fluency. Fluency helps children move from decoding and word recognition to comprehension.

**Comprehension Skills**—Parents and teachers can use rhymes as a leaping-off point for discussions by asking *who, what, where, how,* and *why* questions. This encourages children to recall words and facts from the rhymes. These discussions aid in the development of the higher-level, critical thinking skills necessary to succeed in school/life.

Nursery rhymes can introduce children to different ways of life. Discussions can lead to a variety of topics, including activities children engage in now (soccer, music lessons, dance, etc.) as opposed to long ago (herding sheep, fetching water, etc.). Food comparisons can also be made. We still eat pies, but most of us are not familiar with curds and whey. Discussions may be initiated comparing types of homes (shoe vs. apartment), or furniture (tuffet vs. chair). Safety comparisons can also be explored. For instance, would it be a good idea to jump over a lit candle or to go out alone in search of a lost pet?

# How to Use This Book

The following suggestions work for all the rhymes in this book. Each activity builds on the previous one to encourage and excite emergent readers. First, the rhyme is presented to the whole group in a teacher-directed activity through the mini poster and the action folder. Next, the text is introduced using the sentence strips and the picture cards. Then, the black and white stick puppets and mini books can be created by the students during whole-group time, in small groups, or in centers. To round out the study, oral reenactments of the rhyme, using the full-color stick puppets can be presented in class, and then repeated at home using the students' own versions of the puppets.

## Nursery Rhyme Mini Posters

The beautifully illustrated mini posters can be laminated and displayed in the classroom to initiate discussions (*What do the pictures suggest this rhyme is about? What characters are present? etc.*). Later, add this mini poster to the center for children to view while constructing their own stick puppets and coloring the mini books. Copies may be made for each student to practice reading and tracking. As they learn to "attend to print," many valuable literacy skills develop. Ask the students to point to where they begin reading the text. Make hand pointers for students. Cut out and laminate the hands on page 11. (**Optional:** Attach the laminated hands to craft sticks.) Encourage students to identify spaces between words. They may mark the spaces with their fingers, or by coloring in between the words.

## Nursery Rhyme Action Folders

Nursery rhymes are all about action—an egg falls off a wall, a cat plays a fiddle, a mouse runs up and down a clock, a little girl runs away from spiders, etc. Often, this action is unrealistic, which makes it all the more fun to recite and think about. Imagine being the old woman living in the shoe! Children love nursery rhymes, despite the fact that many rhymes do not make sense in modern-day language.

The action folders included in this book were designed to introduce the selected rhymes. In a sense, the folders set the stage. Illustrated assembly directions are given for each rhyme included in this book. By creating the adorable action folders, children will have a visual to attach to the stories told by the rhymes. In a sense, the folders clarify the stories for the children.

Initially, the folders can be prepared by the teacher and used to present the nursery rhymes in small groups of up to 10 students. Later, an individual folder can be used as a presentation tool to review the rhyme with the whole class. Once the rhyme has been memorized, the folder can be placed in a center where children retell the rhyme and act it out using the folder as a prop. At some point, older children might be assisted in making their own folders using black and white copies of the patterns or their own drawings. This would offer them a creative outlet as well as an opportunity to practice fine motor skills.

For older children, the nursery rhyme action folder can be placed in a writing center. There, the children write stories about the nursery rhyme, create other poems using rhyming words, substitute new words for the rhyme, or create a play using copies of the nursery rhyme characters they have colored and attached to craft sticks. The folders can also be used in a math center where students create word problems generated by the nursery rhymes.

## Sentence Strips

Sentence strips allow teachers to model a variety of crucial reading strategies. The sentence strips included for each rhyme are arranged by phrase to capitalize on the rhyming nature of the poems and to increase oral language skills. Spacing between the words is exaggerated to make the individual words more distinctive for beginning readers. The large print can be easily viewed in pocket charts, on bulletin boards, or on other display areas.

Use the strips to reinforce tracking skills and develop fluency. Display the strips in an appropriate location. Read the rhyme to the students with expression, encouraging them to do likewise. Review the strips on a regular basis to develop fluency and reinforce both top-to-bottom and left-to-right tracking. This repetition leads to *automaticity*—reading that is effortless and automatic. Use a pointer when tracking the words. In the beginning, you may wish to emphasize the space in between words as well.

Use sentence strips as guides when attending to print (reading). Vary the method in which they are used. See which of the shared reading methods listed below is most effective. Change methods from time to time to renew interest in the rhyme.

- **Choral reading**—the whole group reads the rhyme aloud (chanting).

- **Echo reading**—a group leader reads one line at a time, and it is repeated by the students.

- **Silly reading**—the entire rhyme is read in a silly or unusual voice.

- **Whisper reading**—the entire rhyme may be read in a whisper, or start out in a regular voice and get progressively quieter for each line.

- **Alternate reading**—take turns (teacher/students, pairs or groups of students) reading lines.

Once the above activities have been practiced several times, introduce the "Rebuilding Rhymes" task card on page 21. This card can be used with any rhyme in the book. Demonstrate the activity with the students. Model the rebuilding process a number of times before children proceed independently at a center.

## Picture Cards

The picture cards were created to enhance the sentence strips. They can be placed at the ends of the appropriate strips in the pocket chart. Picture cards can also be used for the following activities:

- in place of words in the pocket chart to create "rebus" rhymes.

- as prompts to retell the story, or as story-starters for oral or written activities.

- as flash cards. Lay the cards out word-side-up. Read the word and flip the card over to self-check.

## Word Cards

Make two laminated sets of sentence strips for each rhyme. One set remains in phrases as discussed on page 7. Cut the second laminated set into individual word cards. Use the word cards in conjunction with the task card on page 23, entitled "Missing Words." This card can be used with any rhyme in the book. Model the activity with the students.

The word cards may also be used in the following activities:

- Use the word cards in conjunction with the picture cards created for each rhyme. Match each picture card to the appropriate word card.
- Sort the cards by beginning or ending letters/sounds.
- Sort the cards by long or short vowel sounds.
- Use the cards as flash cards.
- Sort the cards into sets of rhyming words. Later, add other rhyming words to the list.
- Arrange a group of selected cards in alphabetical order.
- Use the cards to rebuild the rhyme, word by word, in a pocket chart.

## Mini Books

Mini books offer students opportunities to practice teacher-modeled reading strategies independently. The more opportunities students have to read, the more their fluency improves. Each nursery rhyme comes with its own mini book. The books vary in length and pages are numbered for easy assembly. Children may color the pages, cut them out, and create their own books to read silently or aloud. Allow time for students to read and re-read the books aloud to a partner, or to a small group. Later, send them home for students to share with their families.

Consider making additional copies of the mini book for use in a center. Before copying the pages, delete the page numbers. Then, mount each page on a separate sheet of construction paper and laminate the cards. Mix up the cards in the center and encourage students to sequence them correctly to retell the rhyme.

## Stick Puppets

There are two sets of puppets for each rhyme. The first set is black and white line art. Copy a set for each student to color, cut out, and assemble. This may be done as a whole class activity or presented in a center after modeling the task card, "Make a Stick Puppet," found on page 19. Students may use the completed puppets to reenact the rhymes. Later, they may use the puppets to create rhymes and stories of their own.

The second set of puppets is a full-color set. This set may be cut out, laminated, and assembled for the teacher to use to share the rhyme. Model appropriate ways to present the rhyme during use in a center. It might be helpful to create a mini-puppet stand and/or puppet theater to enhance puppet show presentations. (See page 9 for directions.)

## How to Make a Puppet Stand

Create a puppet stand/storage container. Use a box with a lid (similar to a shoebox).

### Materials

Hey Diddle, Diddle

- shoebox
- box cutter
- crayons or markers

1. Cut a small slit in the top of the box for each puppet. The craft sticks should fit snuggly in the slits.
2. Label the box with the name of the rhyme. Label the inside of the lid with the number of puppets included in the set. Later, the puppets and a copy of the mini poster may be stored in the stand.

## How to Make a Folding Puppet Theater

Create a portable, freestanding theater to set up on a table (center), or on the floor (impromptu show).

### Materials

- precut foam core display board
- ruler
- pencil
- markers or paint/paintbrush
- duct tape or masking tape
- box cutter

1. Measure and cut an opening (window) in the top half of the center section of the display board.
2. Decorate the front and sides of the board.
3. Use tape to reinforce the inside creases of the board.

## How to Make a Freestanding Puppet Theater

Create a three-sided, freestanding theater to place on a tabletop or counter (center).

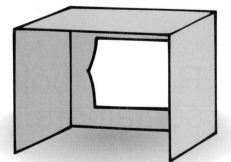

### Materials

- cardboard box
- ruler
- pencil
- paint and paintbrush
- box cutter

1. Cut the bottom and one large side from the box.
2. Measure and cut an opening (window) in the remaining large side.
3. Paint the exterior of the box.
4. If desired, add a curtain on the window.

# Center Rules

1. Respect one another's work.

2. Respect one another's ideas.

3. Take turns.

4. Share.

5. Help one another.

6. Remember with glue—
   A little dab will do!

7. Return tools to their containers.

8. Clean up.

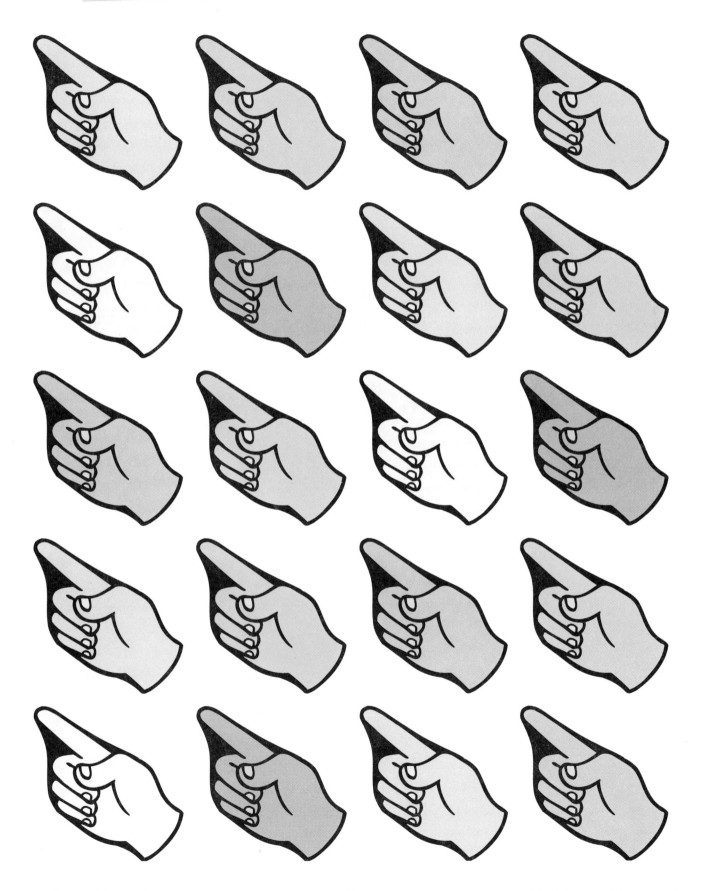

12

# Implementing Center Task Cards

Four student task cards are provided to create four literacy centers. The cards offer generic activities that can be used with each rhyme in the series. The student cards are illustrated and clearly written. Laminate the Center Task Cards for durability. Make certain that the laminated task card and the necessary materials are arranged in the center before it is made available. Model each activity numerous times before students proceed to the center.

The following are presentation suggestions and directions for each literacy center:

## Make a Mini Book

1. Cut out the pages on the dashed lines.
2. Place the title page on top. Make sure the numbered pages are in order.
3. Stack the pages neatly.
4. Staple the pages together.
5. Read the book.
6. Color the book.

## Make a Mini Book

Most young students enjoy making their own books. These mini books are illustrated so that they can be colored easily. Children may add details as time and interest allows. Mini book assembly is the same for each rhyme in this series. Students will need scissors, a stapler, and crayons or markers.

## Mini Book Assembly

1. Review how to hold and use scissors safely. The dashed lines are cut lines. Cut out the title page and the mini book pages for the rhyme.

2. Arrange the pages in order. Check to make sure the title page is on top and the numbered pages follow in the correct order. Point out the page numbers in the dark circles.

3. Stack the pages neatly and staple them together on the left side. If staplers are not available, students may punch holes on the left side of the pages and use rings or yarn to hold them together.

4. Arrange times for students to color their books. This may be done at a center, at their desks, or during free periods.

**Suggestions:** Read the books together. Spend time focusing on the words. Model reading with expression. Point out basic punctuation, if appropriate.

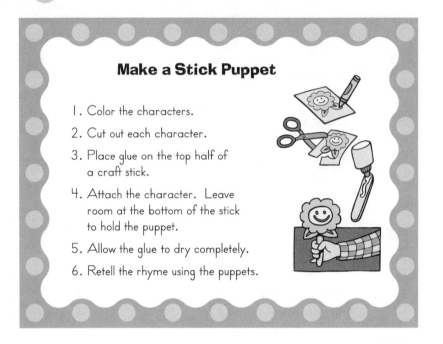

## Make a Stick Puppet

1. Color the characters.

2. Cut out each character.

3. Place glue on the top half of a craft stick.

4. Attach the character. Leave room at the bottom of the stick to hold the puppet.

5. Allow the glue to dry completely.

6. Retell the rhyme using the puppets.

## Make a Stick Puppet

Two sets of stick puppets are provided for each rhyme. The colored set should be laminated for repeated use. It may be used by the teacher to present the rhyme and later placed in a literacy center for students to use to reenact the rhyme. The black and white reproducible set may be copied for students' individual use.

There are two kinds of stick puppets: one-sided puppets and two-sided puppets. In most cases, the two-sided puppets depict opposites (mouse running *up*/mouse running *down*).

1. Review how to hold and use scissors safely. Have students color and cut out the characters.

2. For two-sided puppets, point out the dashed lines. Instruct students not to cut on the dashed lines. Show students how to fold the puppet on the dashed lines.

3. Demonstrate how to affix glue to the top half of a craft stick. Remind students that they want to leave the bottom half of the stick without glue so that they can hold it when reenacting the rhyme. If craft sticks are unavailable, the puppets may be taped to straws.

4. For two-sided puppets, show students how to attach one character to one side of the stick. Then, have students lay the character facedown so the stick is visible. Again, place glue on the top half of the stick. Fold the character pattern over so that the second character covers the glue.

5. Wait until the glue dries to use the puppets. Lay the puppets flat, or press the sticks into lumps of clay.

**Suggestions:** Use the laminated, full-color puppets to demonstrate how the rhymes may be presented. Spend some time demonstrating how to twist a two-sided puppet in one hand. Explain that this will take practice and that it is okay to put the puppet down and flip it over, if necessary.

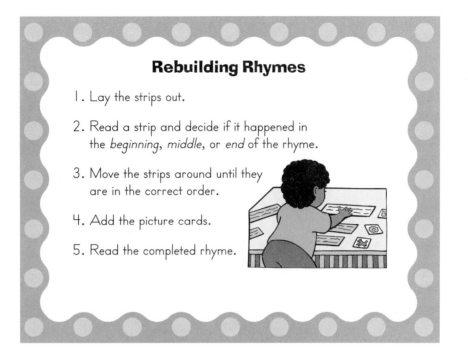

**Rebuilding Rhymes**

1. Lay the strips out.

2. Read a strip and decide if it happened in the *beginning*, *middle*, or *end* of the rhyme.

3. Move the strips around until they are in the correct order.

4. Add the picture cards.

5. Read the completed rhyme.

## Rebuilding Rhymes

By the time students are ready for this literacy activity, they should have had numerous opportunities to see the sentence strips used in pocket charts as part of whole-group, teacher-directed activities. Determine ahead of time if the center will be equipped with a pocket chart, if students will work on a table, or an area of the rug or floor. Factor this decision into the presentation.

1. Discuss the meaning of the terms: *beginning*, *middle*, and *end*. When students understand the difference between the terms, explain that they will be placing sentence strips in order to "rebuild" the rhyme.

2. Hold up a strip and read it to the students or have them read it aloud. Decide when it happened in the rhyme: in the beginning, the middle, or the end. Place the strip accordingly.

3. Continue choosing strips, reading them, determining their order in the rhyme, and putting them in the appropriate place.

4. Add the picture cards once all the strips are placed in order.

5. Read the rhyme together.

**Suggestions:** You may wish to begin this presentation by arranging the strips incorrectly and reading the jumbled rhyme to the students. Ask, "What is wrong with this rhyme?" Once it has been determined that the phrases are out of order, demonstrate how they can be rearranged.

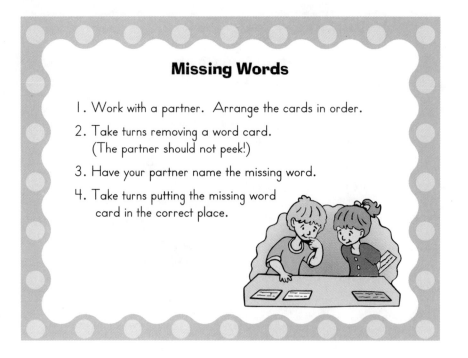

**Missing Words**

1. Work with a partner. Arrange the cards in order.

2. Take turns removing a word card.
   (The partner should not peek!)

3. Have your partner name the missing word.

4. Take turns putting the missing word
   card in the correct place.

## Missing Words

This literacy center activity is great for pairs of students. Decide ahead of time if students will work on a phrase at a time, a sentence at a time, or the whole rhyme. Arrange the center to suit student needs. If students are working in pairs on sentences or phrases, they may trade sets of cards when they finish and repeat the activity.

1. Demonstrate how to lay out all the cards and read them together, as a team.

2. Have one partner close his or her eyes and turn his or her head away as the other partner removes a card.

3. Instruct the partner who removes the card to hold the "mystery" card behind his or her back, or lay it facedown near the other cards.

4. After the card is hidden, the partner with the closed eyes should open them and read the remaining cards to determine which word card is missing.

**Suggestions:** Determine ahead of time if students will leave a space where the missing card was taken, or if they will rearrange the cards to fill the empty slot. More advanced students can be instructed to pull a noun card or a verb card.

**Note:** Prior to any center activity, spend time discussing appropriate center behavior. A Center Rules poster is provided on page 10.

# Make a Mini Book

1. Cut out the pages on the dashed lines.

2. Place the title page on top. Make sure the numbered pages are in order.

3. Stack the pages neatly.

4. Staple the pages together.

5. Read the book.

6. Color the book.

18

# Make a Stick Puppet

1. Color the characters.

2. Cut out each character.

3. Place glue on the top half of a craft stick.

4. Attach the character. Leave room at the bottom of the stick to hold the puppet.

5. Allow the glue to dry completely.

6. Retell the rhyme using the puppets.

20

# Rebuilding Rhymes

1. Lay the strips out.

2. Read a strip and decide if it happened in the *beginning*, *middle*, or *end* of the rhyme.

3. Move the strips around until they are in the correct order.

4. Add the picture cards.

5. Read the completed rhyme.

# Missing Words

1. Work with a partner. Arrange the cards in order.

2. Take turns removing a word card. (The partner should not peek!)

3. Have your partner name the missing word.

4. Take turns putting the missing word card in the correct place.

# Hey Diddle, Diddle

Hey diddle, diddle,
the cat and the fiddle,

the cow jumped
over the moon.

The little dog laughed
to see such sport,

and the dish ran away
with the spoon!

# Hey Diddle, Diddle

## Literacy Skills Activities

**Phonemic Awareness**—Have the students name each word in the rhyme that begins with the "d" sound (*diddle, dog, dish*). Ask them to list other words they know that begin with the "d" sound. Then, instruct the students to name each word in the rhyme that begins with the "s" sound (*see, such, sport, spoon*). Finally, ask them to name other words that begin with the "s" sound.

**Phonics**—Create word families. Substitute beginning consonants (onsets) for the "d" in *dish* and the "sp" in *spoon*. Ask the students what the pattern (rime) is in each family (*ish, oon*). With the aid of your students, extend the word families by going through the alphabet and adding "silly" words to the lists (*bish, mish,* or *foon, zoon*).

**Vocabulary Development**—What is a *fiddle*? A fiddle is a type of violin: a stringed, musical instrument. Have each student use the word *fiddle* in a sentence and illustrate the sentence.

Ask students what you call someone who plays a fiddle? (fiddler) What do you call someone who teaches? (teacher) swims? (swimmer) dances? (dancer)

**Fluency**—Performance reading requires practice. Practice builds fluency, and helps develop student confidence. Set aside time for students to practice reading their mini books. When comfortable, provide an audience and offer students opportunities to performance read.

**Comprehension Skills**—Have students make a list of all the "action words" in the rhyme (*jumped, see, laughed, ran*). Explain that action words are called "verbs." Have students stand up and act out the rhyme, paying special attention to the action words. Ask students what other action words they know that could be added to the list. (**Hint:** Remind students ahead of time to run in place, not around the classroom.)

## Cross-Curricular Activities

**Social Studies**—The dish and the spoon ran away. Talk about "running away." Is it a good idea? Discuss safety rules; later brainstorm a list of safety rules for the home, classroom, or playground.

**Math**—Talk with students about things that come in pairs in the rhyme (*cat and fiddle, dish and spoon*). Who are some characters in other rhymes that come in pairs (*Jack and Jill, Mary and her lamb*)? What are some other items that come in pairs (*salt and pepper, shoes, socks, eyes, ears, etc.*)? Later, have the students count by two's.

**Science**—Talk about the moon. Draw different phases of the moon. Discuss with students the name for each phase and why it might have been given that name (*new moon, gibbous moon, full moon, crescent moon*).

**Movement/Drama**—Create an obstacle course or circuit. Encourage students to do some of the same activities suggested by the action words in the rhyme. For example, have students jump seven times over chalk X's on the ground or carpet, do two rolling laughs (on a mat), run to the other end of the area, and sit down. For the return trip, change the number of times they do each task.

# Redo the Rhyme

**Directions:** Cut out the pictures at the bottom of the page. Create a new rhyme by adding the pictures to the boxes. Read your new rhyme to a friend.

## Hey Diddle, Diddle

Hey diddle, diddle, the [    ] and the fiddle,

the [    ] jumped over the moon.

The little [    ] laughed to see such sport,

and the [    ] ran away with the spoon!

28

# Hey Diddle, Diddle

## Materials

- file folder (option: use a dark color)
- scissors and ruler
- glue and clear tape
- tagboard
- green construction paper
- drinking straw
- ⅛" hole punch
- 2 brads
- string
- patterns on pages 31–33 and copy of mini poster (page 25)

## Construction

1. Glue a copy of the nursery rhyme mini poster to the back of the file folder. Label the folder tab.

2. Cut out the cat and the musical notes, the moon, the cow, the dish with the spoon, and the dog.

3. Cut strips of green construction paper to use for grass.

4. Open the file folder and glue the grass along the bottom of the folder. Glue the cat to the lower left corner of the folder.

5. Glue the moon to the top left side of the folder. Position the moon pattern 2½" (6.5 cm) from the top and 3½" (9 cm) from the center of the folder.

6. Glue the dog to the lower left corner of the right side of the folder. Add the musical notes between the dog and the cat.

7. Laminate the folder.

8. Glue the cow and the dish with the spoon to pieces of tagboard (for durability) and cut them out. Laminate the cow and the dish with the spoon separately.

9. Cut the drinking straw to make a 3" (7.5 cm) piece. Punch a hole into each end of the straw using the hole punch.

10. Punch a hole in the lower center of the cow and poke a hole below the moon. (See illustration on page 30.) Attach the cow to one end of the straw using one of the brads and attach the other end of the straw to the hole below the moon (on the folder) using the other brad.

# Hey Diddle, Diddle

## Construction *(cont.)*

11. Once the cow is attached to the file folder, make certain it can move back and forth easily over the moon. If not, loosen the brads and try again.

12. Punch a hole in both sides of the dish.

13. Cut a piece of string 9" (23 cm) long and insert it through the holes in the dish, making sure the string is on the back side of the dish.

14. Measure 2" (5 cm) up from the bottom of the folder on the right side. Punch a hole 2" (5 cm) from the center of the folder, and punch a hole 1" (2.5 cm) from the right side | of the folder.

15. Take the string with the dish and spoon and thread the ends of the string in each hole. Secure the string with tape on the back of the folder.

16. Once the dish with the spoon is attached to the folder, make certain it can move back and forth easily. If not, remove the string and try again.

# Hey Diddle, Diddle

## Action Folder Patterns

32

# Hey Diddle, Diddle

## Action Folder Patterns

34

# Hey Diddle, Diddle

Hey diddle, diddle,
the cat and the fiddle,

1

the cow jumped over the moon.

The little dog laughed to see such sport,

**2**

and the dish ran away with the spoon!

**3**

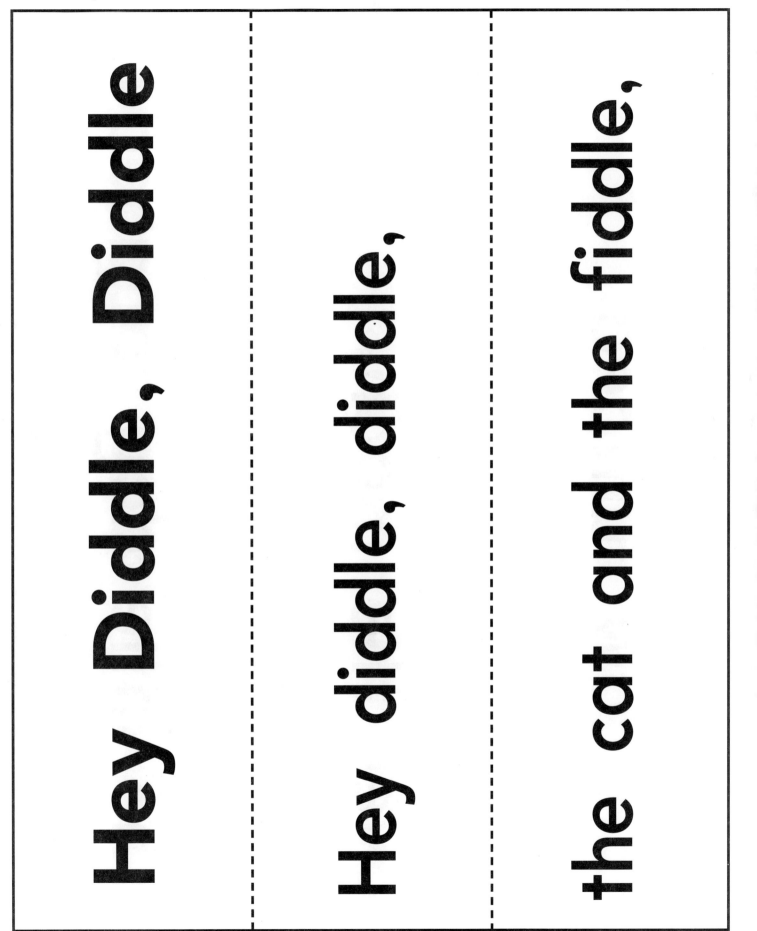

Hey Diddle, Diddle,

Hey diddle, diddle,

the cat and the fiddle,

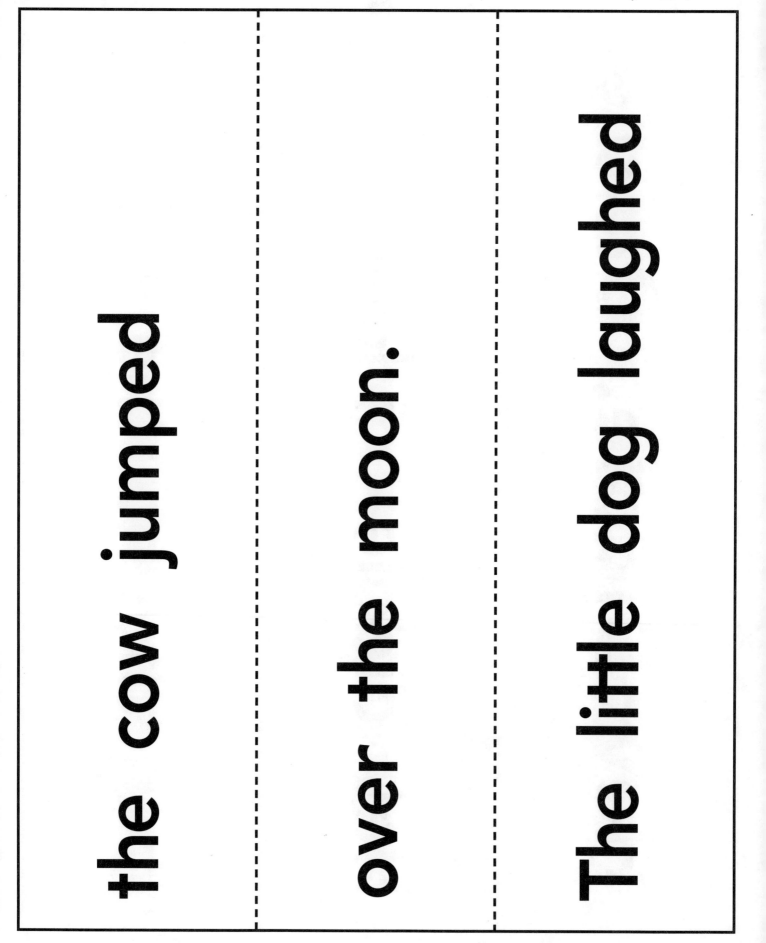

the cow jumped

over the moon.

The little dog laughed

to see such sport,

and the dish ran away

with the spoon!

# Hey Diddle, Diddle

40

# Hey Diddle, Diddle

42

# Hey Diddle, Diddle

# Hey Diddle, Diddle

dog

cat and fiddle

moon

cow

spoon

dish

# Humpty Dumpty

Humpty Dumpty sat on a wall.

Humpty Dumpty had a great fall.

All the king's horses

and all the king's men

couldn't put Humpty

together again!

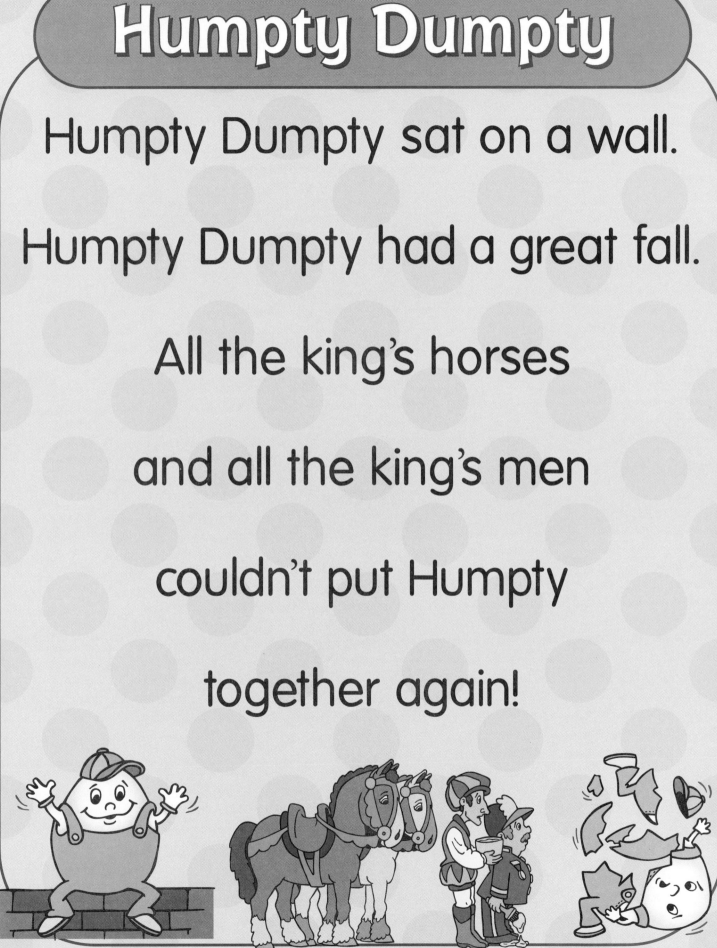

46

# Humpty Dumpty

## Literacy Skills Activities

**Phonemic Awareness**—Provide counting cubes or discs for each student. Say a word from the rhyme. Have students repeat the word and then segment the word into sounds (phonemes). Instruct them to indicate the number of sounds for each word with the cubes and identify the different sounds. For instance, *wall* will have three cubes—w–a–ll. *Men's* will have four cubes—m–e–n–s.

**Phonics**—Focus on word family patterns from the rhyme. Create a chart using the following word patterns from the rhyme: **-all, -at.** Later, enlist the students' help in adding words not found in the rhyme.

**Vocabulary Development**—What is a *king*? A king is a ruler or leader of a country. Have students name some kings they know (*Old King Cole*).

Ask students if there are words in the rhyme that are nonsense words (*Dumpty*) and why they are in the poem (*to help it rhyme*). Can you think of another rhyming last name for Humpty (*Humpty Bumpty*)?

**Fluency**—Focus on the punctuation in the rhyme. Discuss the exclamation point with students. Ask them what the voice should do when there is an exclamation point (rise with enthusiasm). Have students practice reading the rhyme with expression.

**Comprehension Skills**—Encourage students to retell the saga of Humpty Dumpty. Have them include the following: Who are the main characters? What is the problem in the rhyme? How does the story end? Why was it difficult to put Humpty together again? What is an alternate ending?

## Cross-Curricular Activities

**Social Studies**—Ask students who tried to help Humpty Dumpty (*king's horses and king's men*). If Humpty Dumpty were to fall today, who might come to take care of him (*doctor, ambulance*)?

Humpty Dumpty lived in a land where a king was the ruler. Ask students who the leader is in our country. What would you do if you were the ruler of our country?

**Math**—Fill large plastic eggs with items that can be sorted. Give each student a filled egg to open and sort. Have him or her create and illustrate math problems to show what was in the egg (*example: 3 red buttons, 2 blue buttons, and 1 black button = 6 buttons*).

**Science**—With the students' help, create a list/collage of animals that lay eggs (*lizards, chickens, ducks, snakes, birds, fish, insects, turtles, some dinosaurs*).

Have students collect pictures of animals and sort them into two piles: those that hatch from eggs and those that do not hatch from eggs. Discuss with students that eggs provide protection for young animals.

**Movement/Drama**—Have a Humpty Dumpty Egg Toss. Line children up in two lines, facing each other in pairs. Give each child on one side a hard-boiled egg (or beanbag) and have him or her toss it to the partner. If a pair misses, it steps out of the line. Pairs who catch the egg take a step back and toss again. Repeat the process until only one team is left.

**Alternative:** Have the children toss plastic eggs into a basket.

# Cracked Shell Puzzle

**Directions:** Cut out the pieces and put them together. What is the picture on the puzzle? Glue the puzzle to a sheet of construction paper and color it.

# Humpty Dumpty

## Materials

- light blue file folder
- scissors
- glue
- clear tape
- brad
- tagboard
- ⅛" hole punch
- ruler
- patterns on pages 51–61 and copy of mini poster (page 45)

## Construction

1. Glue a copy of the nursery rhyme mini poster to the back of the file folder. Label the folder tab.

2. Cut out the three red brick wall patterns. (One of the patterns [b] is a two-sided pattern.)

3. Open the file folder and glue two brick walls (a & c) across the bottom of the folder. Make sure the two walls meet in the middle (crease) of the folder. Save the two-sided wall (b) for later.

4. Cut out the horses and the king's men. Glue the horses and the men to the middle of the wall on the right side of the folder.

5. Laminate the folder.

6. Cut out both pieces of Humpty Dumpty. For durability, glue the pattern pieces to tagboard and cut them out.

7. Laminate both pieces of Humpty Dumpty and the double-sided wall.

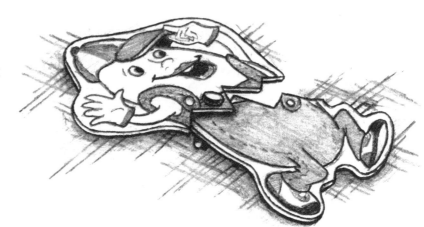

# Humpty Dumpty

## Construction *(cont.)*

8. Using the hole punch, punch a hole on the dot in the top half of Humpty Dumpty and a hole on the dot in the bottom half of Humpty Dumpty.

9. Punch another hole on the left side of the file folder. This hole should be located in the middle of the folder, 4½" (11.5 cm) from the top above the wall.

10. Press a brad through the top of Humpty Dumpty where indicated. Then, press the brad through the bottom half of Humpty Dumpty so that the character is complete.

11. Attach Humpty Dumpty to the folder using the brad. Secure the back of the brad with clear tape.

12. Once Humpty Dumpty is attached to the folder, make sure he moves smoothly. If not, loosen the brad and try again.

13. Take the double-sided brick wall and place it on top of the wall on the right side, covering up the horses and the king's men. Attach the wall to the right side of the folder using clear tape.

14. Place tape on either side of the wall where it connects to the folder. This will create a hinge.

15. Once the wall is attached to the folder, make certain it can open and close. If not, take off the tape and try again.

**Presentation Note:** When saying the line, *Humpty Dumpty fell off the wall*, move the central wall pattern behind Humpty Dumpty's legs and let the two sections separate to indicate that he is falling.

# Humpty Dumpty

## Action Folder Patterns

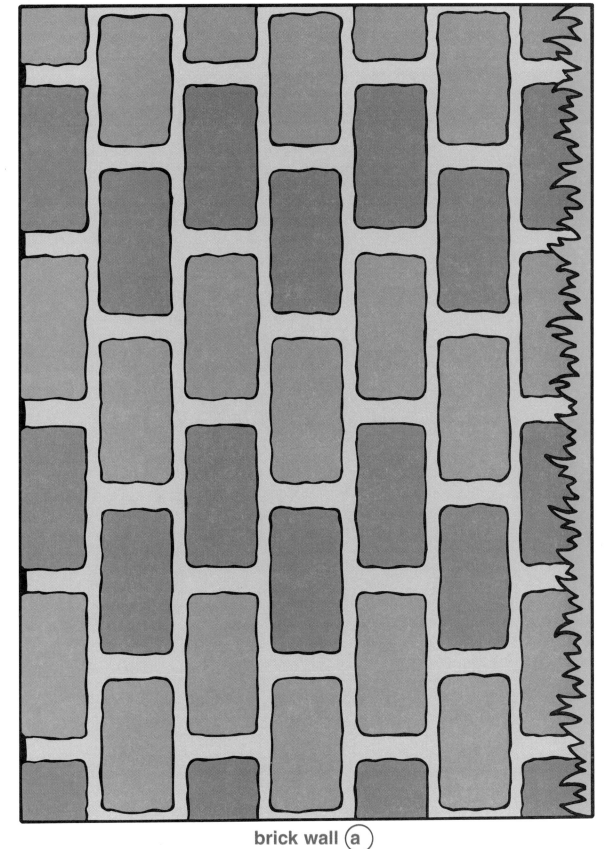

brick wall (a)

# Humpty Dumpty

## Action Folder Patterns

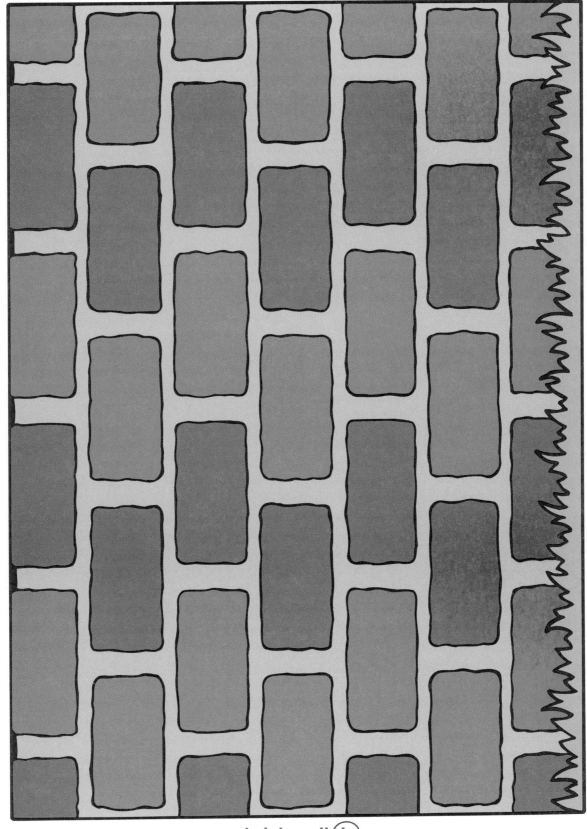

brick wall (b)

# Humpty Dumpty

# Humpty Dumpty

## Action Folder Patterns

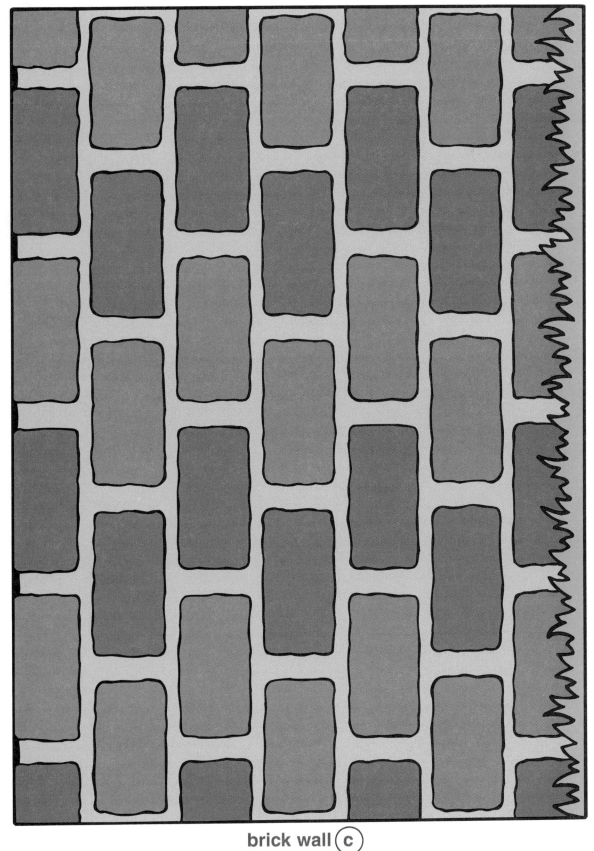

brick wall (c)

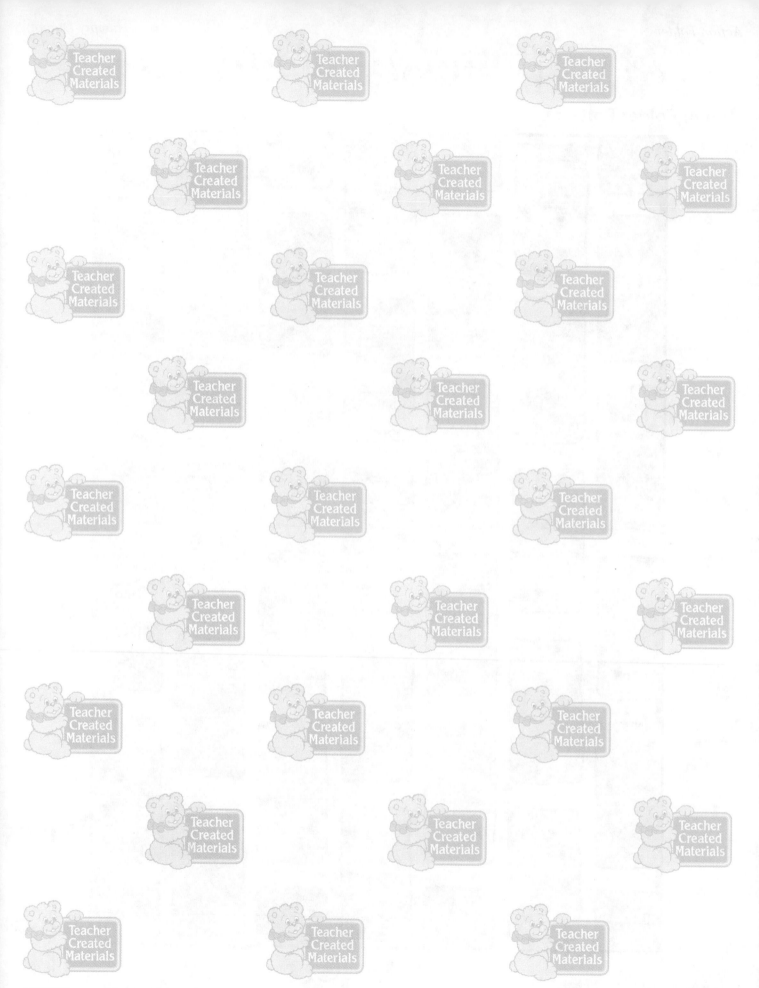

56

# Humpty Dumpty

## Action Folder Patterns

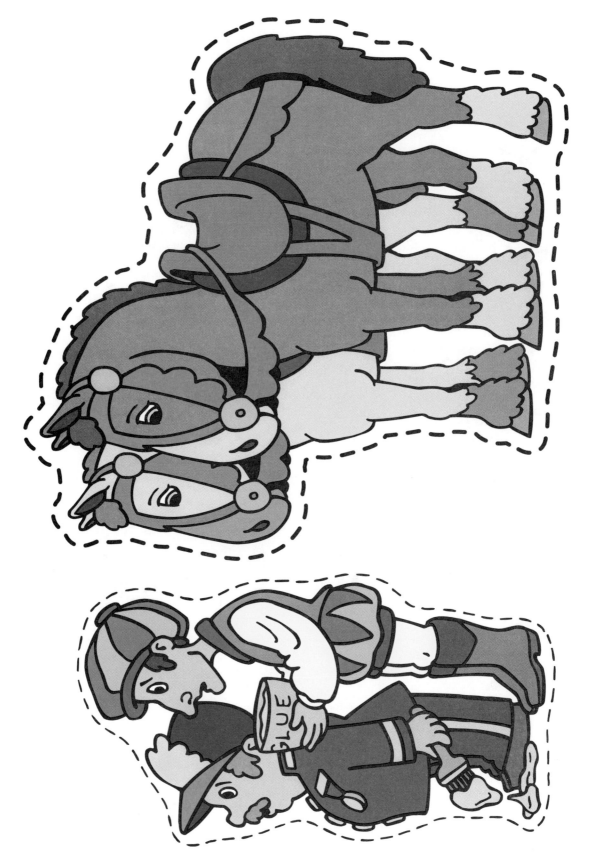

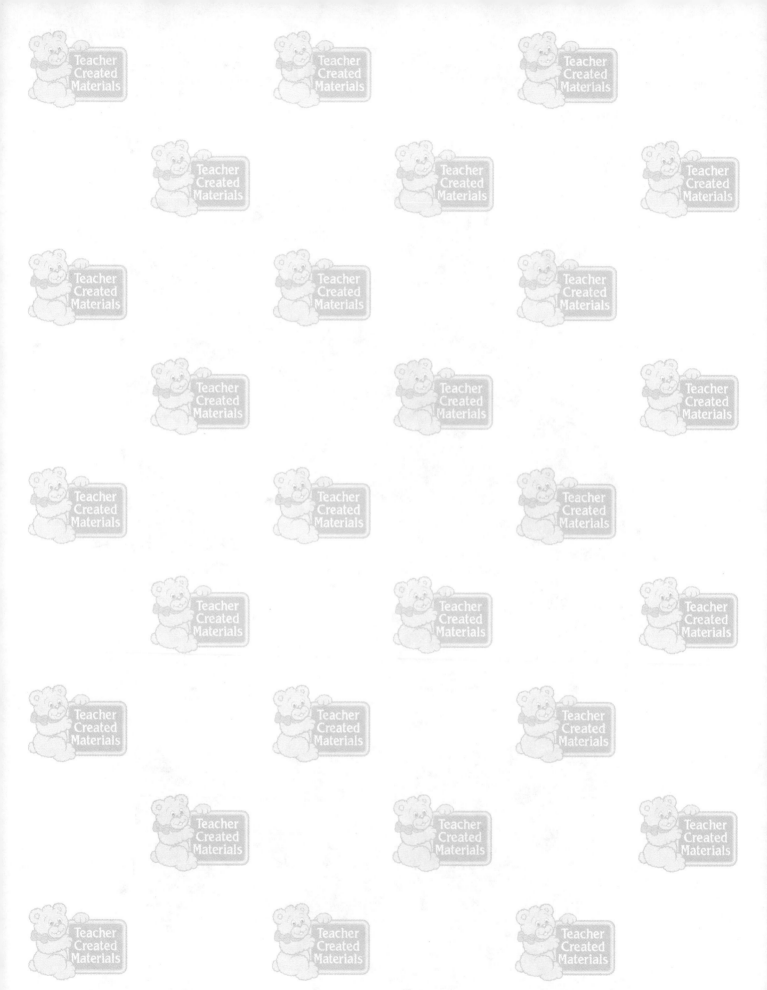

# Humpty Dumpty

**Action Folder Patterns**

## Action Folder Patterns

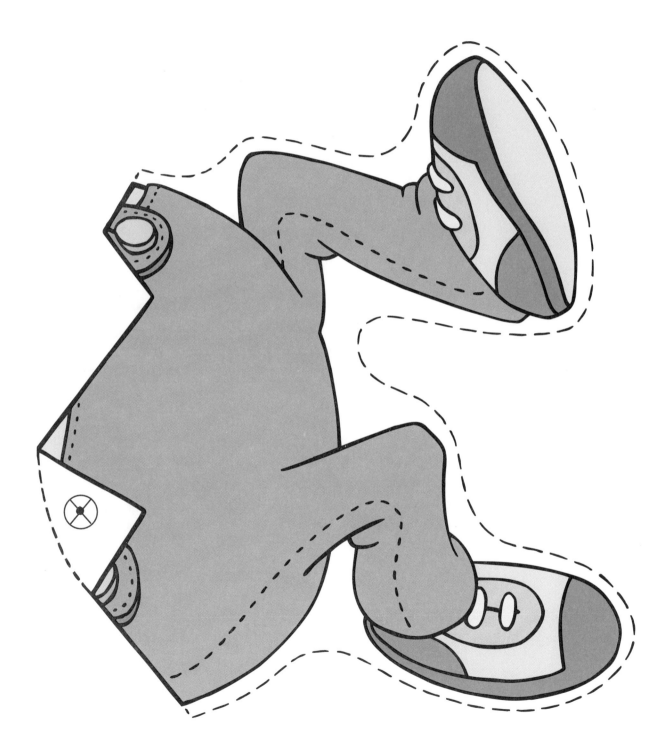

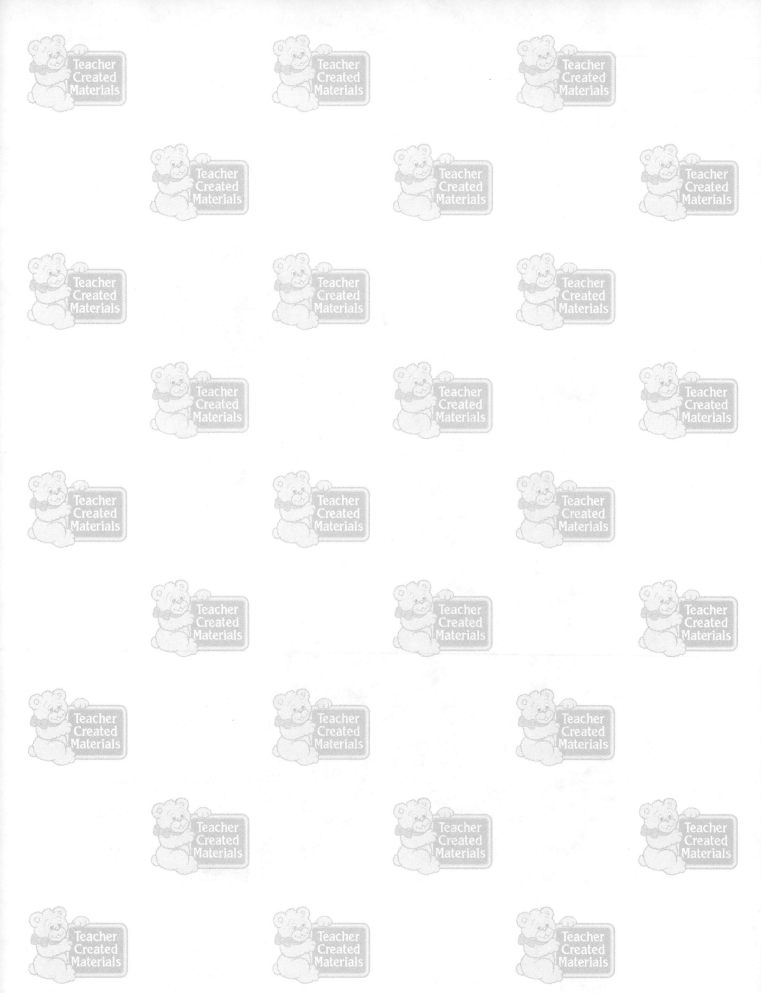

**Humpty Dumpty**

Humpty Dumpty sat on a wall.

1

Humpty Dumpty had a great fall.

**2**

All the king's horses

**3**

and all the king's men **4**

couldn't put Humpty together again! **5**

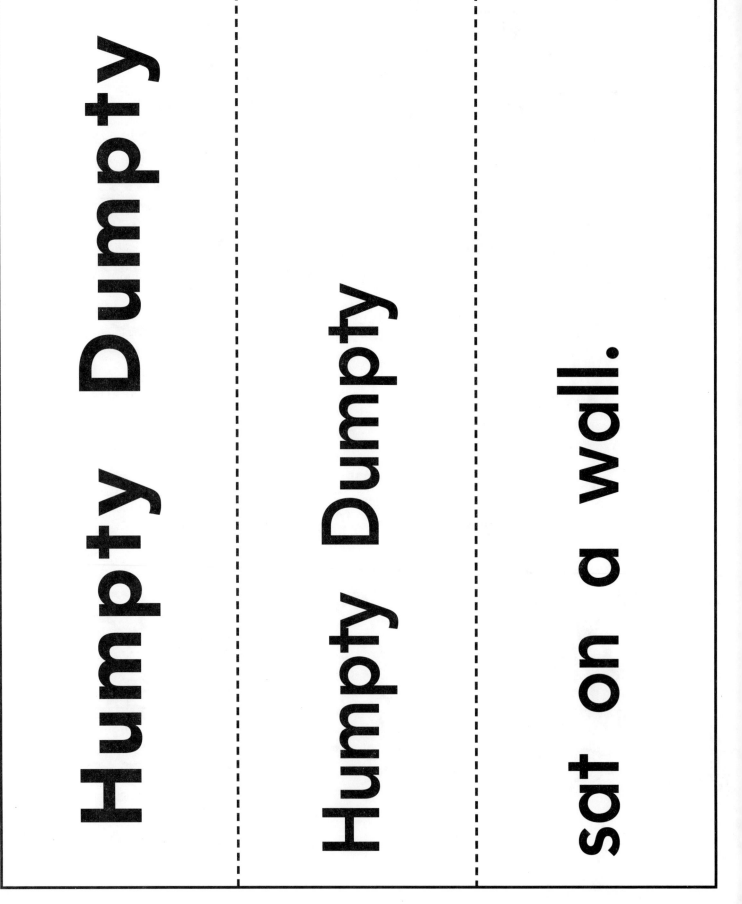

**Humpty Dumpty**

**Humpty Dumpty**

**sat on a wall.**

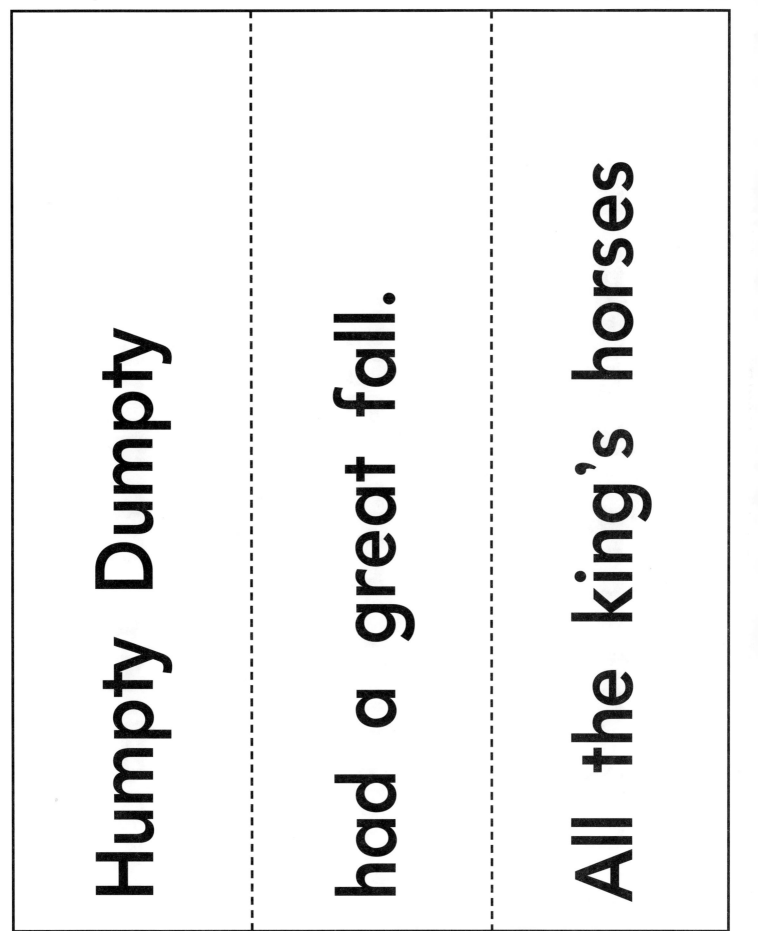

Humpty Dumpty

had a great fall.

All the king's horses

and all the king's men

couldn't put Humpty

together again!

# Humpty Dumpty

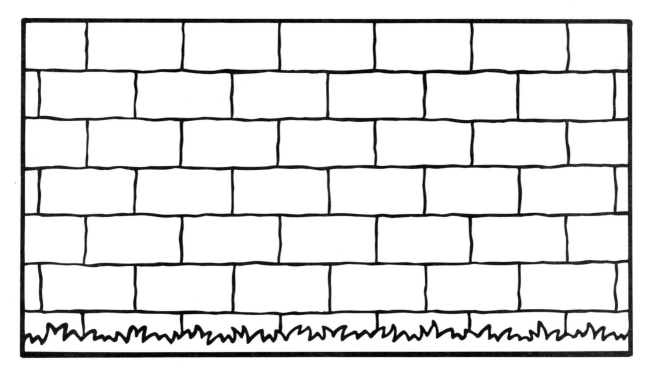

# Humpty Dumpty

# Humpty Dumpty

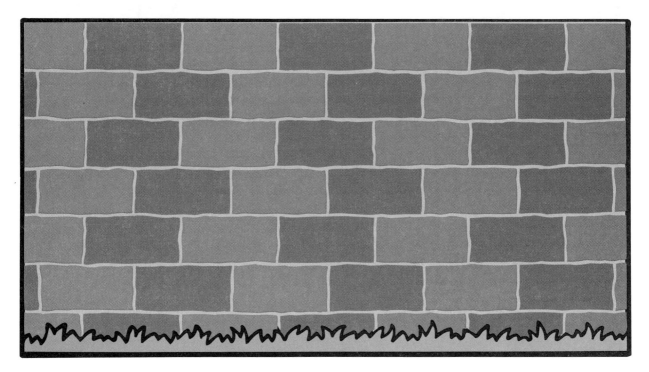

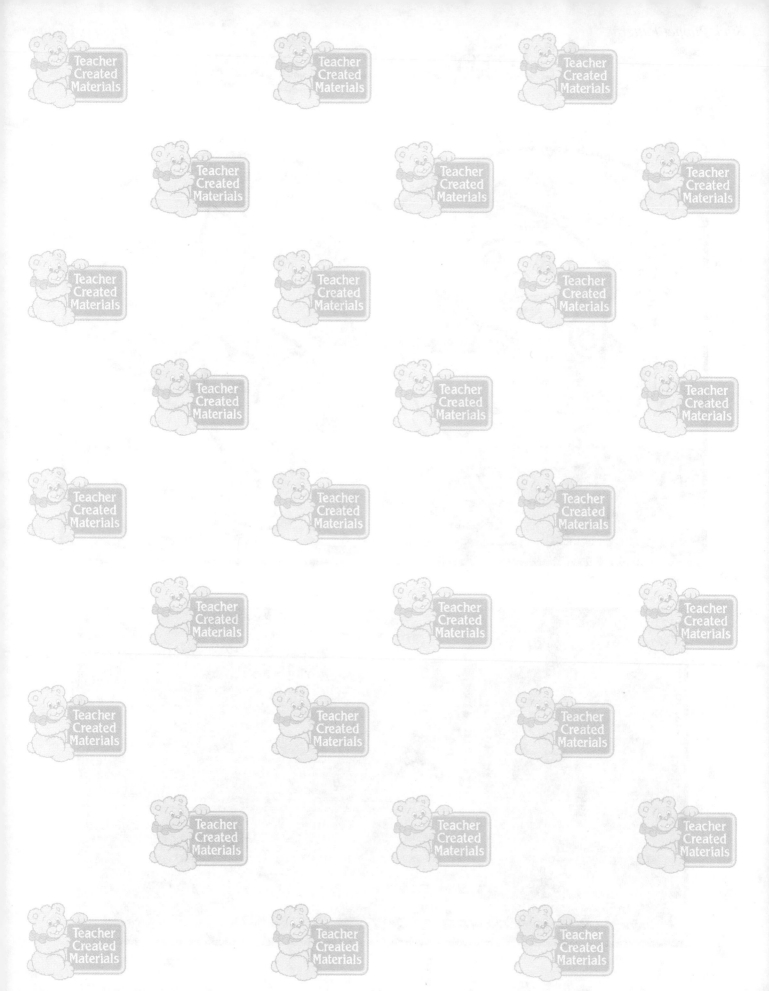

72

# Humpty Dumpty

74

# Humpty Dumpty

# Humpty Dumpty

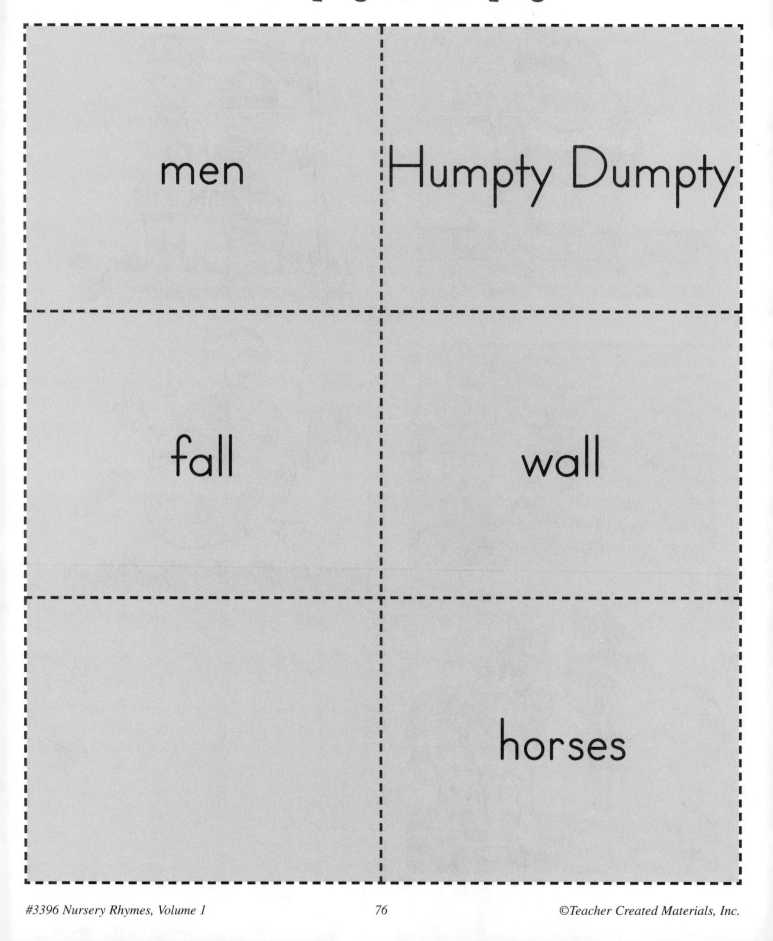

men

Humpty Dumpty

fall

wall

horses

# Little Bo-Peep

Little Bo-Peep
has lost her sheep,
and doesn't know where
to find them.
Leave them alone,
and they'll come home,
wagging their tails
behind them.

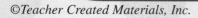

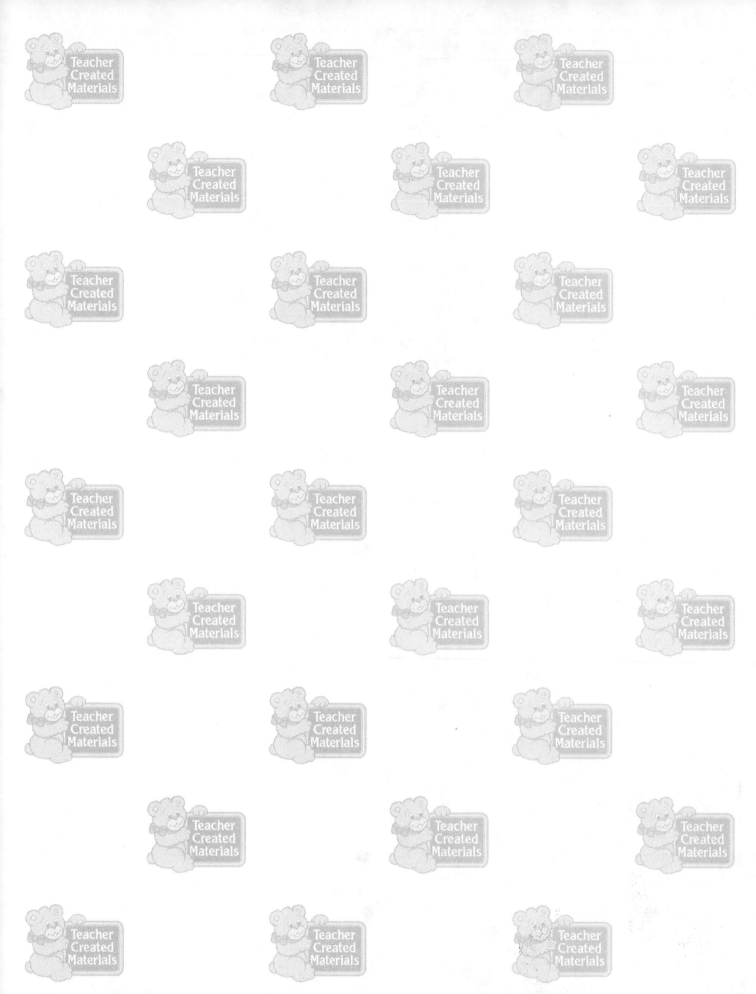

78

# Little Bo-Peep

## Literacy Skills Activities

**Phonemic Awareness**—The word *sheep* contains the phoneme /sh/. This is an example of one sound represented by two different letters (digraph). Have students name other words that contain the "sh" sound (*sheet, share, shine, brush, wash, wish*). Point out that sometimes "sh" is at the beginning of a word and sometimes it is at the end of the word. Ask students to tell whether the "sh" sound is at the beginning or end of each word.

**Phonics**—Many of the words in this rhyme are spelled phonetically. Focus on the words where the letter/sound correspondence is one to one (*has, lost, and, find, wag*). Have children write the dictated words. Review the correct spelling immediately and correct any errors.

**Vocabulary Development**—Ask children what a *shepherd* does. A shepherd is a person who takes care of sheep. He guides them to and from the grazing areas and protects them. (Do they see the connection?—Sheep-herder.)

**Fluency**—Make copies of the mini poster for each student and provide crayons or markers. Have them read along with you as you read the rhyme with expression. Then, focus on the individual words of the rhyme. Have students mark or color the space in between each word in the rhyme.

**Comprehension Skills**—Little Bo-Peep has a problem. (*She can't find her missing sheep.*) Have students name the problem and discuss the suggested solution. Who might have made the suggested solution? What is another suggestion for Little Bo-Peep?

There are opposites in the rhyme (*lost and found*). Ask the children, "What are opposites?" Have them list other words they know that are opposites.

## Cross-Curricular Activities

**Social Studies**—Little Bo-Peep lost her sheep. Discuss what students would do if they were lost. What would they do if they lost a pet? Guide students toward safe solutions (*practice calling 911, learn home address and phone number as well as a non-family member to call in an emergency, etc.*).

**Math**—Have students practice addition and subtraction using cotton balls for manipulatives. Instruct them to make up different problems to solve. (*Little Bo-Peep had nine sheep. She lost two sheep. How many sheep does she have left?*)

**Science**—Ask the children why the sheep wagged their tails when they returned. What other animals can wag their tails (*dog, cat, raccoon, etc.*)? Have students help make a chart listing different animals and the different uses for their tails. (*Fish and sea mammals maneuver with their tails. Squirrels use their tails for balance and to keep warm. Monkeys and opossums use their tails to grasp things.*)

**Movement/Drama**—Allow the students to play Hide and Seek. When found, have them make sounds like a sheep or lamb. Make a variation of Pin the Tail on the Donkey. Draw a large outline of a sheep. If time allows, have children paint the sheep with glue and cover it with cotton balls. Make tails using black or white construction paper. Finally, have students play Pin the Tail on the Sheep.

# Long E Sheep

**Directions:** Look at the sheep. Each one has a picture on it. Color the picture if it has a long "e" sound. Cross out each picture that does not have the long "e" sound.

# Little Bo-Peep

## Materials

- file folder
- scissors
- glue
- clear tape
- patterns on pages 83–89 and copy of mini poster (page 77)

## Construction

1. Glue a copy of the nursery rhyme mini poster to the back of the file folder. Label the folder tab.

2. Cut out the patterns.

3. Glue the sun to the top right corner of the folder.

4. Glue Little Bo-Peep (and her hill) to the left side of the folder. The right side of the hill should align with the crease in the folder.

5. Add flowers to the folder at the base of the hill on both sides.

6. Attach the hill pattern with the frolicking sheep to the right side of the folder. The left side of the hill should align with the crease in the folder.

7. Place one bird above the hill on each side of the folder.

8. Laminate the folder.

9. Glue the three sheep to the back (green side) of the remaining hill pattern. Laminate this pattern separately.

10. Lay the laminated hill pattern on top of the hill in the folder. Align the two patterns at the crease. The flower-covered hill should cover the hill with the sheep.

# Little Bo-Peep

## Construction *(cont.)*

11. Using clear tape, attach the flat edge of the flower hill to the center fold of the file folder. Place the tape on either side of the hill to create a flap. (See illustration.)

12. Once the hill is attached to the folder, make sure it opens and closes easily. If not, remove the tape and try again.

# Little Bo-Peep

**Action Folder Patterns**

# Little Bo-Peep

**Action Folder Patterns**

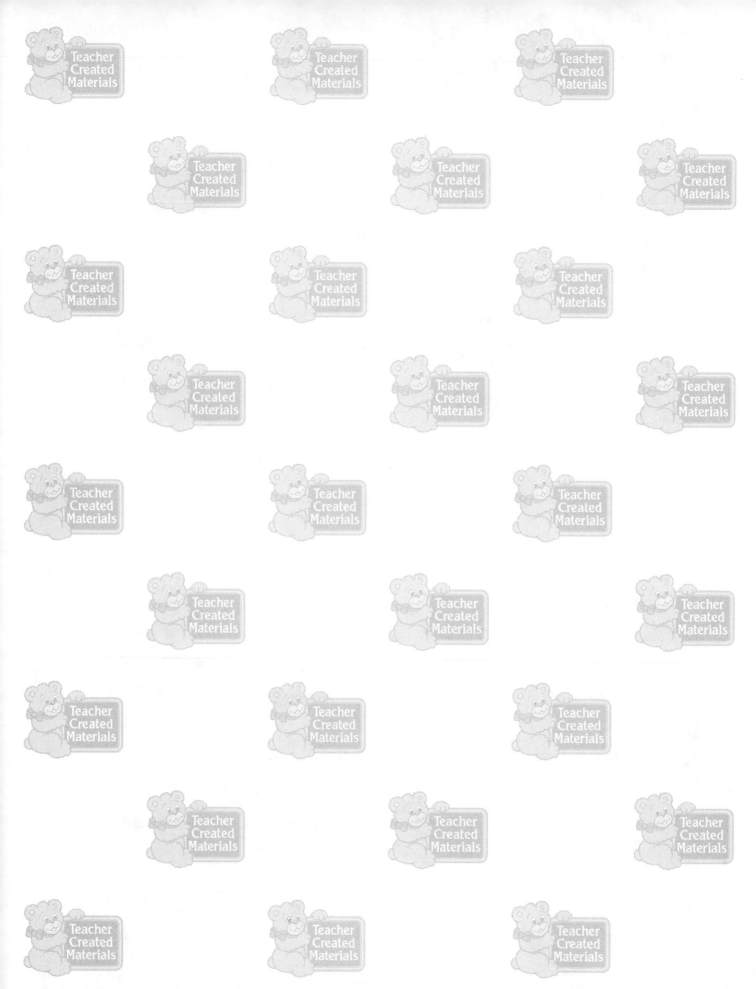

# Little Bo-Peep

## Action Folder Patterns

# Little Bo-Peep

# Little Bo-Peep

## Action Folder Patterns

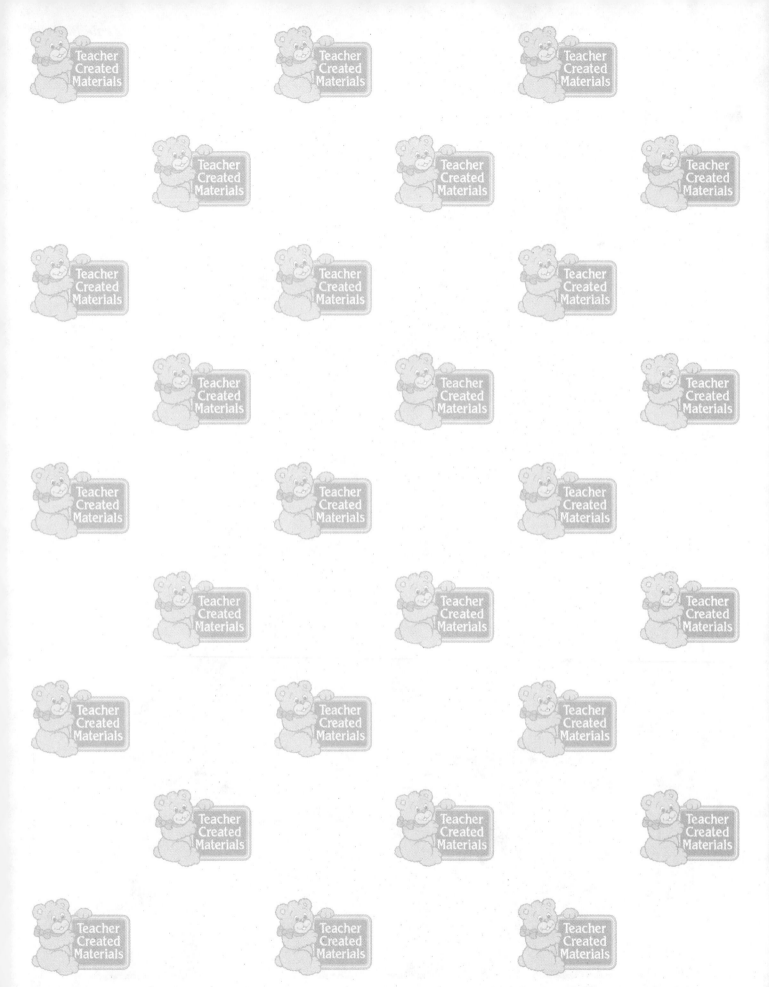

# Little Bo-Peep

Little Bo-Peep has lost her sheep,

**1**

and doesn't know where to find them. **2**

Leave them alone, and they'll come home, wagging their tails behind them. **3**

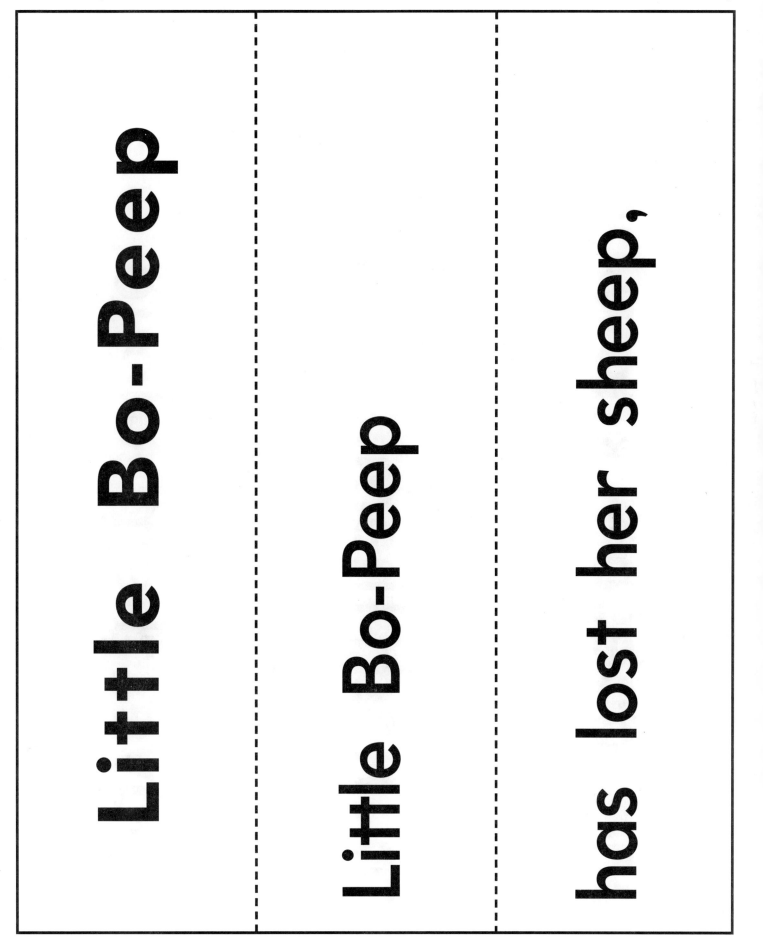

**Little Bo-Peep**

**Little Bo-Peep**

**has lost her sheep,**

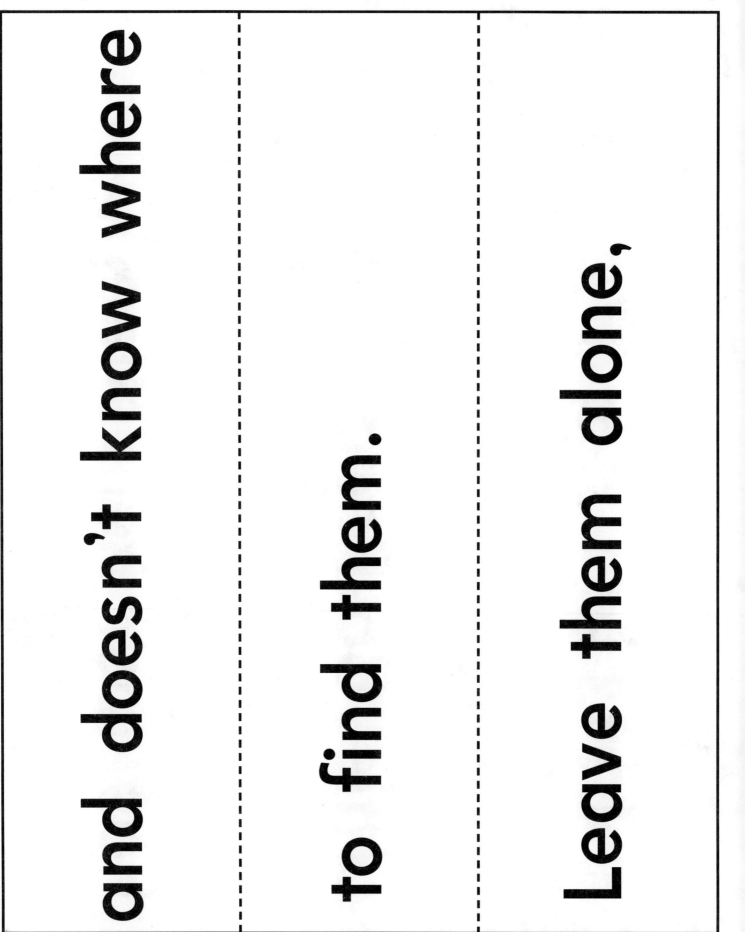

and doesn't know where

to find them.

Leave them alone,

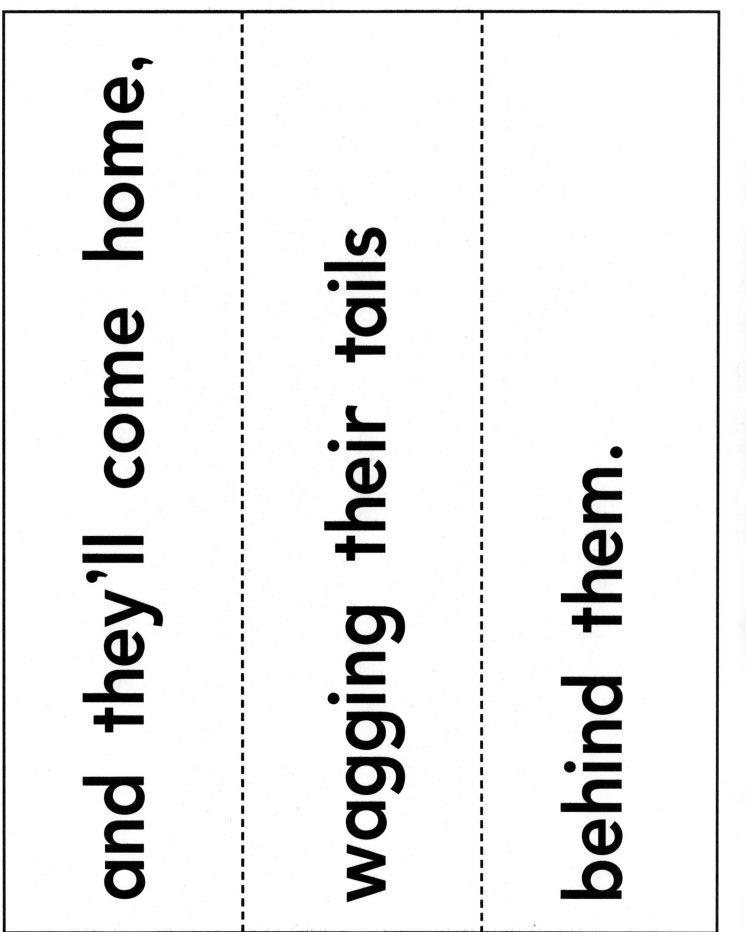

**and they'll come home,**

**wagging their tails**

**behind them.**

# Little Bo-Peep

**Note:** Point out to children that each two-sided puppet demonstrates an opposite.

# Little Bo-Peep

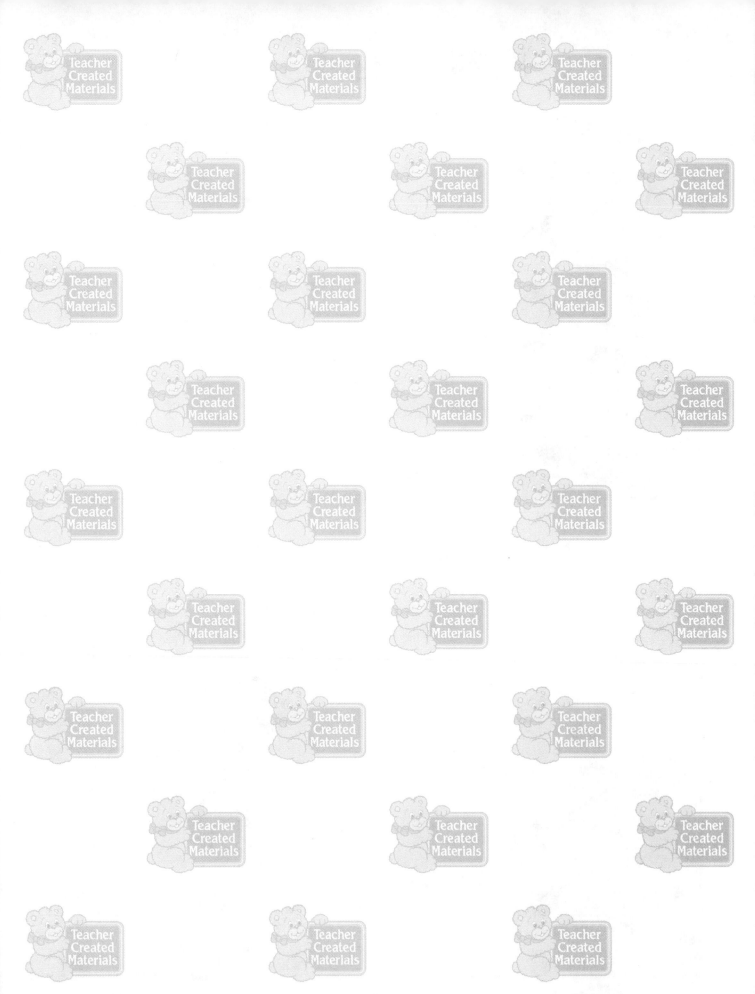

98

# Little Bo-Peep

# Little Bo-Peep

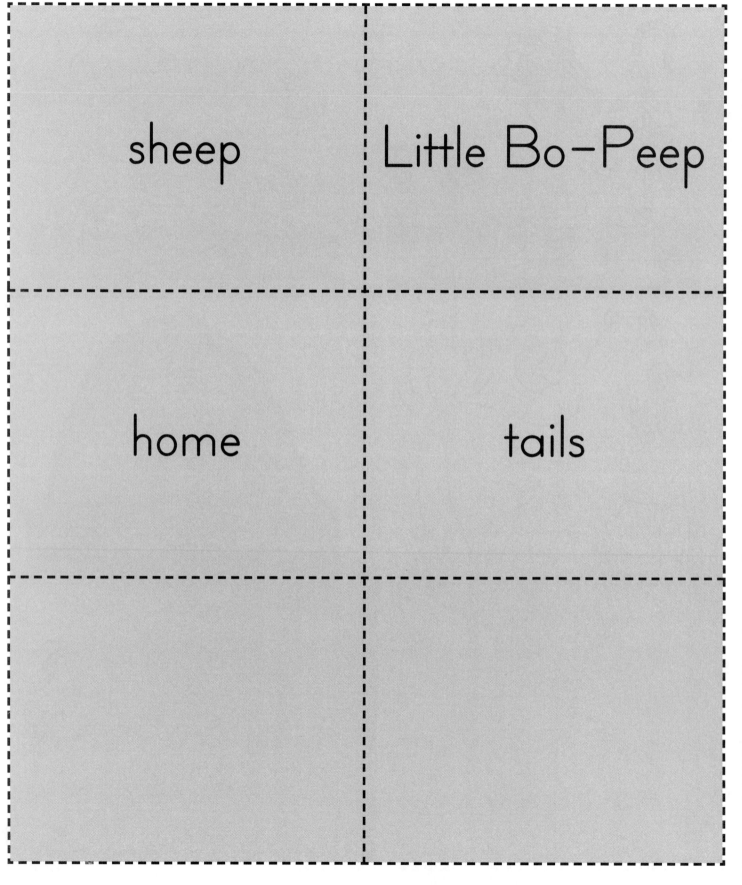

sheep

Little Bo-Peep

home

tails

# There Was an Old Woman

There was an old woman,

who lived in a shoe.

She had so many children,

she didn't know what to do.

She gave them all broth

without any bread.

Then kissed them all soundly

and put them to bed.

102

# There Was an Old Woman

## Literacy Skills Activities

**Phonemic Awareness**—Have children listen for the "w" sound as you read the nursery rhyme aloud. The first time it is read, have them listen only for the sound (*was*, *woman*, *without*, *what*—don't use *who*). The second time the rhyme is read, have students signal the "w" sound with the following hand sign: "Cross your thumb over your pinky finger and hold up the middle three fingers. Doesn't it look like a **W**? Hold your hand up high when you hear the 'w' sound."

**Phonics**—Arrange the first four lines of the rhyme in a pocket chart. (Use the word cards, not the sentence strips.) Read the rhyme aloud. Have students rearrange the words in each line of the pocket chart. Then, read the new nonsense rhyme.

**Vocabulary Development**—The old woman lived in a shoe. Ask students what kind of houses they live in, or wish they could live in. How many kinds of homes can they list (*apartment*, *house*, *castle*, *mobile home*, *tent*, *trailer*)? Write each type of house on a separate word card and place it in a column in a pocket chart. Have students help to arrange the new vocabulary words in alphabetical order.

**Fluency**—Model reading the rhyme using different voices and different intonations. First, read it in a whisper—pretend the children are asleep. Then, try reading it in a scary voice or a deep voice. Ask students, "In how many different types of voices can the rhyme be read?"

**Comprehension Skills**—Ask students, "Why didn't the old woman know what to do? "(*She had so many children.*) "What did she do?" (*She fed them, kissed them, and put them to bed.*)" What else could she have done?" (*Taught them to cook, etc.*)

## Cross-Curricular Activities

**Social Studies**—Discuss with students the possibility of living in a shoe. What would be the positive aspects of living in a house that looked like a giant shoe? What would be the negative aspects of living in a shoe?

Have the children collect pictures of homes and compare the different types.

Have each child learn his or her own address. Encourage the child to write it down.

**Math**—As a class, sort and graph a collection of shoes by color or style.

Have each student measure distances using his or her shoes. How many shoes is it from one end of the classroom to the other? How many shoes tall is the trash can? How many shoes tall is the teacher?

As a class, compare sizes using shoes. Which shoe is the largest, smallest? What can be found that is smaller or larger than the shoe?

**Science**—The old woman's shoe was full of children. Discuss the concept of *full/empty.* Set up a water or bean pouring table for students to use to demonstrate full and empty.

**Movement/Drama**—Practice different expressions. First use only the face. Later add body motions as well *(happy, concerned, sad, frustrated).*

# How Many Children?

**Directions:** Count the children in each picture.  Circle the correct number of children in each box.

# There Was an Old Woman

## Materials

- file folder
- scissors
- glue
- tape or stapler
- tagboard (brown)
- ruler
- patterns on pages 107–113 and copy of mini poster (page 101)

## Construction

1. Glue a copy of the nursery rhyme mini poster to the back of the file folder. Label the folder tab.

2. Cut out the pattern pieces.

3. Glue the tree trunk to the left side of the folder. The bottom of the trunk should touch the bottom of the folder. Attach the treetop to the trunk. (Make certain the apples are pointing in the right direction.)

4. Glue the nest of birds to the tree where the top meets the trunk.

5. Glue the squirrel to the right side of the tree at the base. Glue the tulips to the left side of the tree.

6. Position the blue bird so that it is in the treetop above the nest.

7. Glue the pink bird on the top right side of the folder as if it is flying back to the tree.

8. Glue the interior shoe pattern (with the old woman) to the bottom right side of the folder. Make certain it is to the right of the folder crease.

9. Glue the grouping of children toward the top right corner of the right side of the folder.

# There Was an Old Woman

## Construction *(cont.)*

10. Cut out the boot pattern with the chimney and cut out the center of the window. After the boot is laminated, it will look like a window with glass.

11. For durability, glue the boot with the chimney to tagboard and cut it out.

12. Cut out the window in the boot with the chimney. When laminated, this will look like a windowpane.

13. Laminate the folder and the exterior shoe pattern separately.

14. Attach the exterior shoe pattern to the laminated folder above the interior shoe pattern. Make certain that the old woman and her children are visible through the window. To attach the top shoe, create a hinge using tape on either side of the top of the shoe.

15. Once the top shoe is attached, make certain it can open and close with ease. If not, reattach the tape in a different manner.

# There Was an Old Woman

## Action Folder Patterns

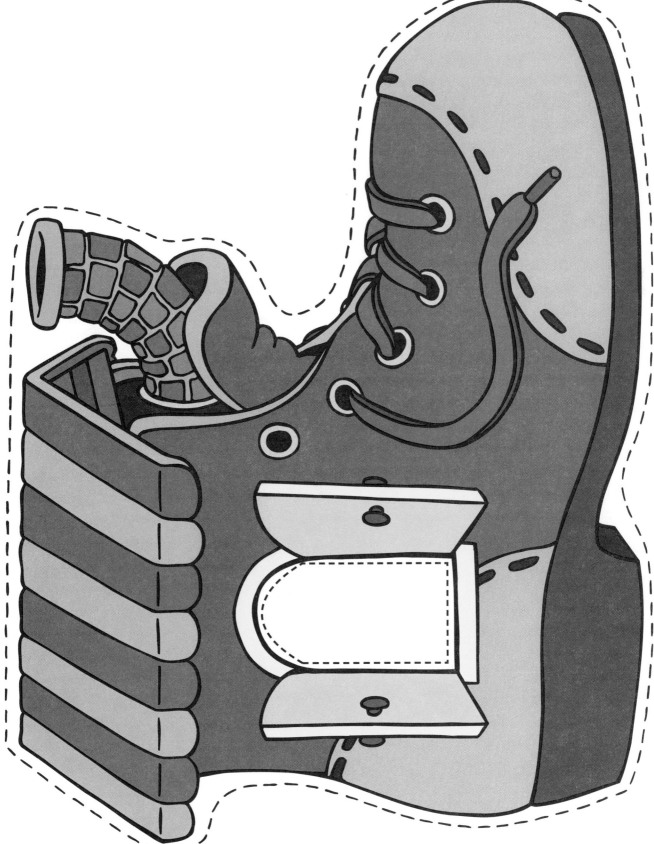

# There Was an Old Woman

**Action Folder Patterns**

# There Was an Old Woman

**Action Folder Patterns**

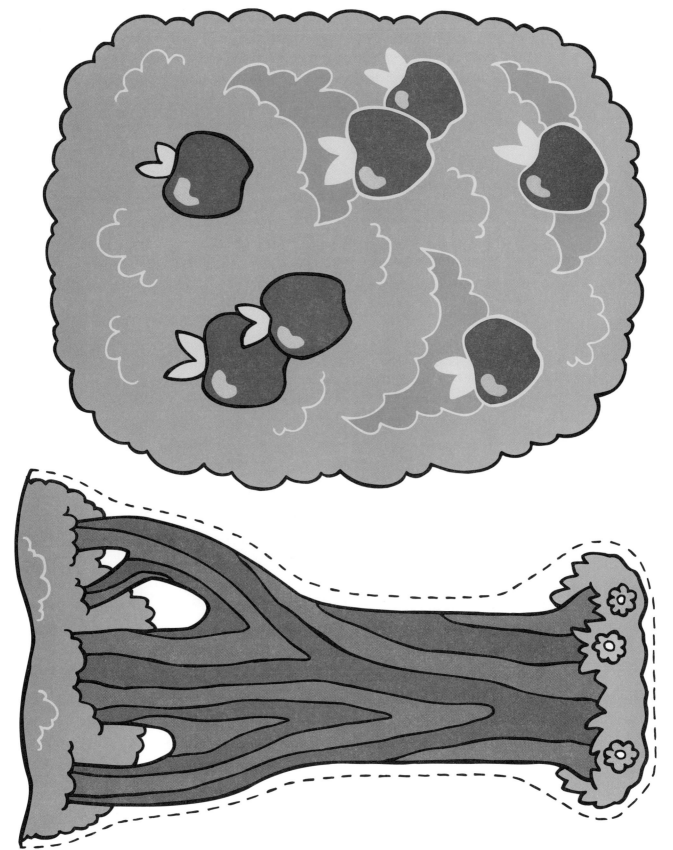

# There Was an Old Woman

## Action Folder Patterns

There was an old woman,
who lived in a shoe.

She had so many children,
she didn't know what to do.

**2**

She gave them all broth
without any bread.

**3**

Then kissed them all soundly   **4**

and put them to bed.   **5**

There was an

Was an

Old Woman

There was an old woman,

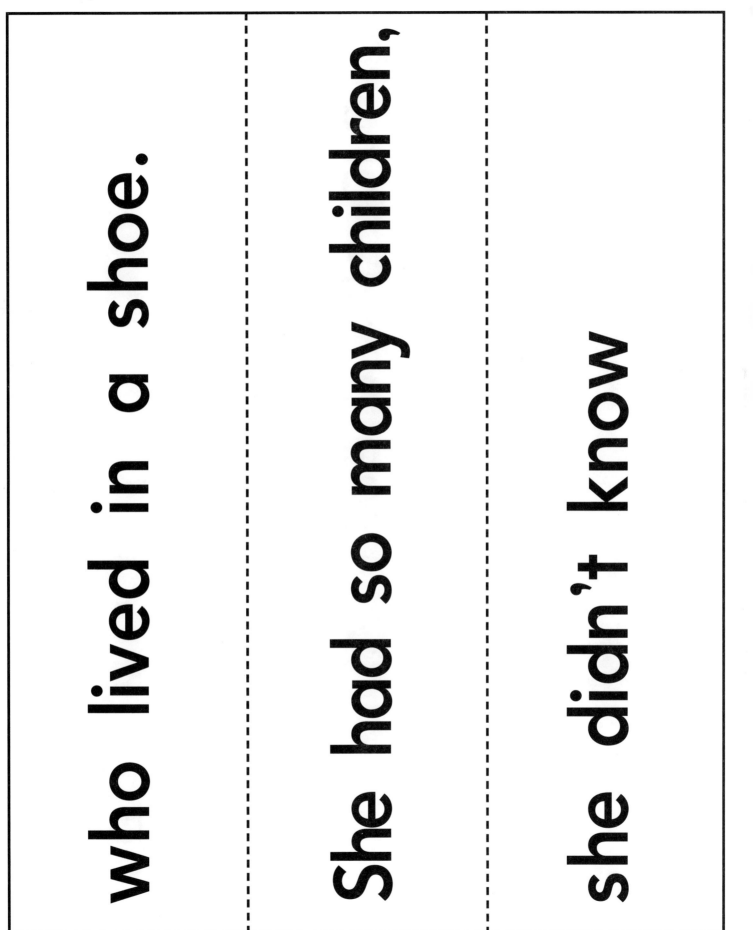

who lived in a shoe.

She had so many children,

she didn't know

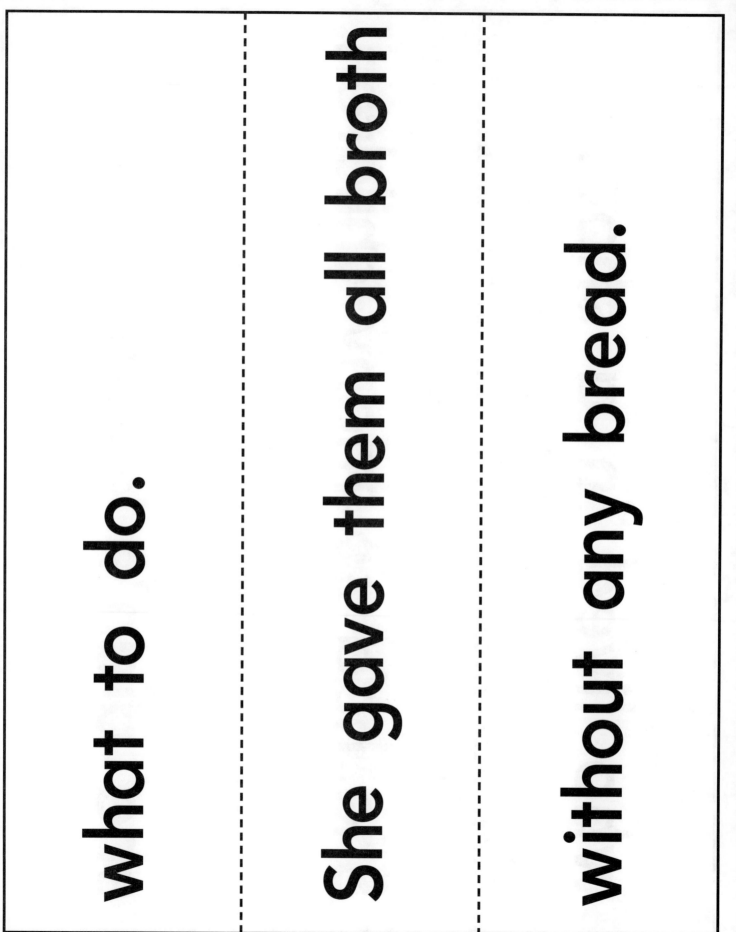

what to do.

She gave them all broth

without any bread.

Then kissed them all

soundly

and put them to bed.

# There Was an Old Woman

122

# There Was an Old Woman

# There Was an Old Woman

# There Was an Old Woman

| | |
|---|---|
| shoe | woman |
| broth | children |
| bed | bread |

# Hickory, Dickory, Dock

Hickory, dickory, dock,

the mouse ran up the clock.

The clock struck one,

and down he run,

hickory, dickory, dock.

# Hickory, Dickory, Dock

## Literacy Skills Activities

**Phonemic Awareness**—Ask the students to listen to the title of the rhyme. Then ask, "Do you hear the "k" sound? Where do you hear the sound? In *hickory* and *dickory*, the "k" sound is in the middle of the word. In *dock*, the "k" sound is at the end of the word. Which words have the "k" sound at the beginning (*kiss, king, kick, etc.*)?"

**Phonics**—Have students list words that rhyme with the word *clock* (*sock, dock, rock, knock, block, lock, stock*). Then ask them to make a list of other pairs of rhyming words from the rhyme.

**Vocabulary Development**—What is a *pendulum*? On a clock, a pendulum swings back and forth beneath the clockworks to regulate the time. Have students swing their arms back and forth like a pendulum. Then ask them, "What else moves back and forth like a pendulum?" (*Swings on a swing set, a metronome.*)

Have each child find words in the rhyme that are on the class word wall and list them on a sheet of paper.

**Fluency**—Divide the readers into two groups. Have them alternate reading lines of the nursery rhyme aloud. Later, break into smaller groups and have each group read a different line. Then, rearrange the students and have them read different lines.

**Comprehension Skills**—Focus on opposites and/or spatial concepts including *up, down, over, under, on,* and *off.* Have students take turns placing a stuffed mouse or a picture of a mouse in different positions. Place the mouse *on* the table, *under* a desk, *over* someone's head, *up* on the top shelf, *down* on the bottom shelf, etc.

## Cross-Curricular Activities

**Social Studies**—Discuss with children why it is important to know what time it is (*in order to get to school, work, meals, or appointments on time*). What would happen if everyone did things when they felt like it, instead of following a schedule?

With the aid of your students, make a list of different methods used to tell time (*clock, sun dial, watch, sun, stopwatch*). Collect pictures and make a time collage.

**Math**—Discuss with students the different ways in which time is marked (*24 hours in a day, 7 days in week, 4 seasons in a year, etc.*).

Have children practice using a stopwatch. Compare how long it takes to complete certain simple tasks.

**Science**—Share non-fiction books about mice. With ideas from the students, create a KWL (**K**now, **W**ant to know, **L**earned) chart to input information about the small rodents.

Have students compare clocks (*grandfather, digital, wind-up, battery-operated, sundial*). Then have them try to take different types of clocks apart to see how they work.

**Movement/Drama**—Encourage children to move their arms in a variety of ways—*up* over their heads, *down* to their toes, *clockwise* and *counter-clockwise, under* their chins, *behind* their backs, etc.

# The Clock Struck One!

**Directions:** Fill in the numbers on the clock face. Draw an hour hand and a minute hand to show one o'clock.

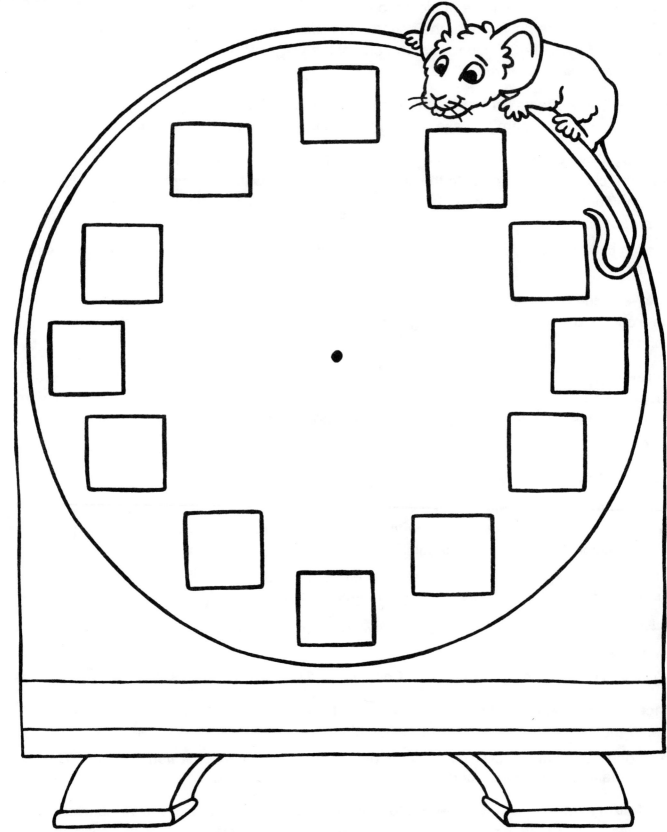

# Hickory, Dickory, Dock

## Materials

- file folder
- scissors
- glue
- hole reinforcements
- tagboard
- ⅛" hole punch
- 15" (38 cm) string
- clear tape
- ruler
- patterns on pages 133–137 and copy of mini poster (page 127)

## Construction

1. Glue a copy of the nursery rhyme mini poster to the back of the file folder. Label the folder tab.

2. Cut out the clock top, the clock bottom, the two mice, and the clock face.

3. Open the folder and turn it lengthwise so that the tab of the folder is at the top.

4. Glue the clock to the folder making sure that the top and the bottom meet at the crease of the folder. Glue the clock face on the clock.

5. Laminate the folder. Laminate the two mice separately.

6. Fold the two mice as shown. Glue the "tail halves" together.

7. Using the hole punch, punch a hole above the front feet of the mouse patterns as marked.

8. Reinforce the holes using tape or hole reinforcers.

# Hickory, Dickory, Dock

## Construction *(cont.)*

9. Punch two holes on the right side of the file folder. One hole should be approximately 3" (8 cm) from the bottom of the folder and 2" (5 cm) from the right side of the folder. The other hole should be approximately 2" (5 cm) from the right side of the folder and 4" (10 cm) from the top of the folder.

10. Thread the piece of string through the hole in the mouse, making sure the string is on the backside of the mouse.

11. Put the ends of the string (with the mouse on it) in each hole in the file folder. Secure the ends of the string with clear tape on the back of the folder.

12. Once the mouse is attached, make certain it can move up and down easily along the side of the clock. If not, remove the string and try again.

**Presentation Note:** Before reciting the rhyme, make sure the mouse is at the base of the clock in the upward position. While saying the line, *The mouse ran up the clock,* move it up the clock. While saying the line, *and down he run*, flip the mouse over in the downward position and move it down the clock.

# Hickory, Dickory, Dock

## Action Folder Patterns

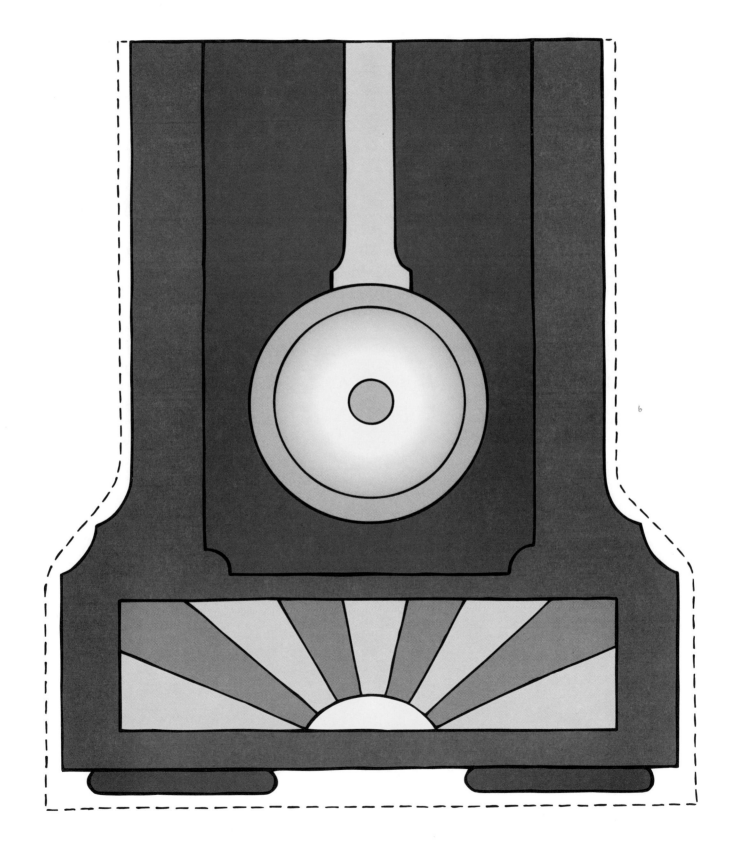

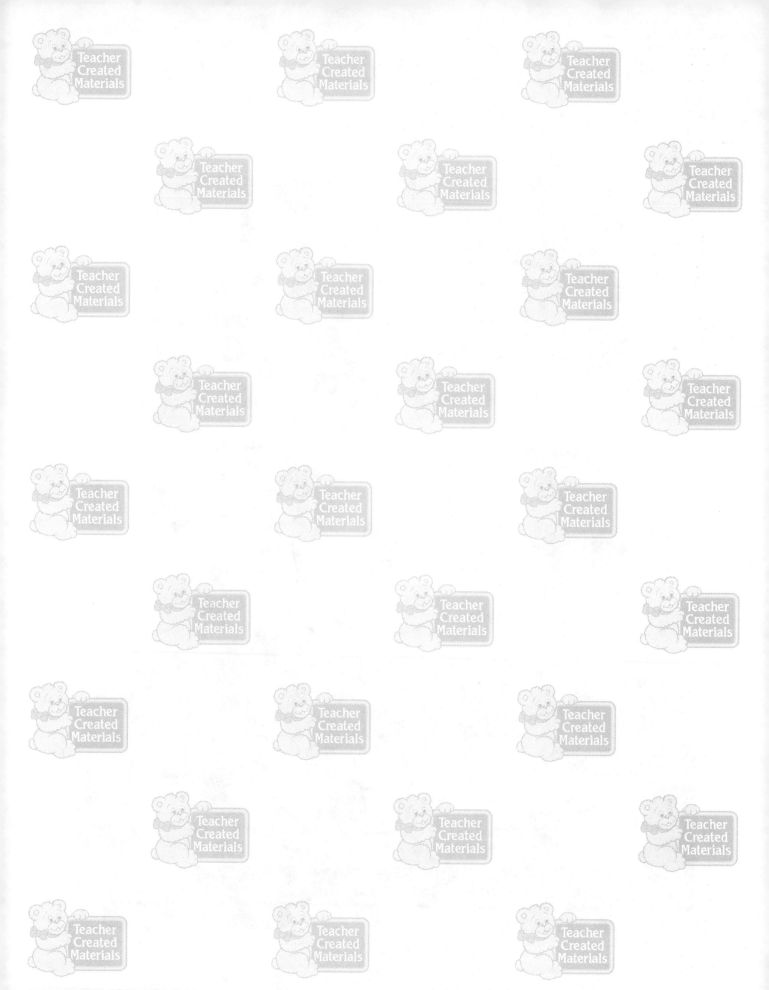

134

## Action Folder Patterns

136

## Action Folder Patterns

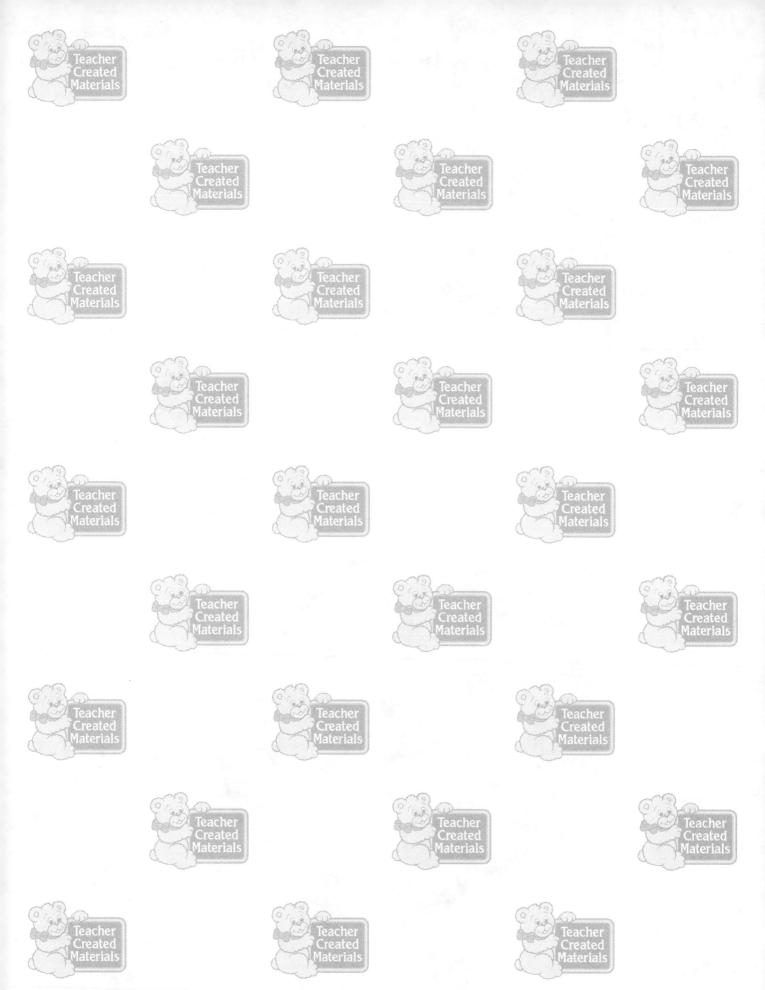

138

# Hickory, Dickory, Dock

Hickory, dickory, dock,
the mouse ran up the clock.

1

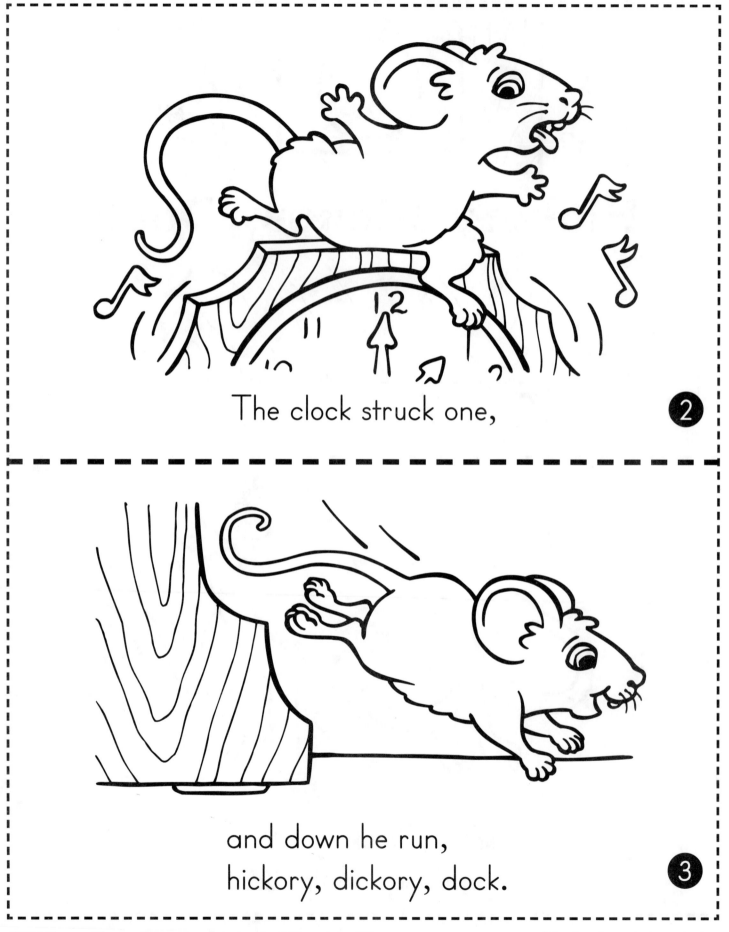

The clock struck one,

**2**

and down he run,
hickory, dickory, dock.

**3**

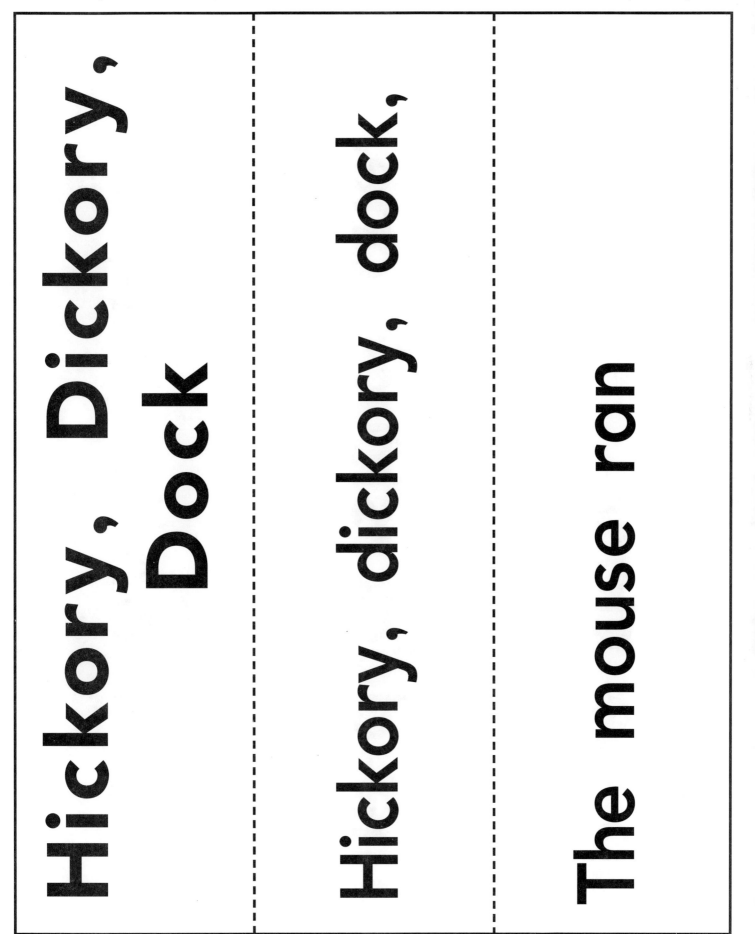

Hickory, Dickory, Dock

Hickory, dickory, dock,

The mouse ran

up the clock.

The clock struck one,

and down he run,

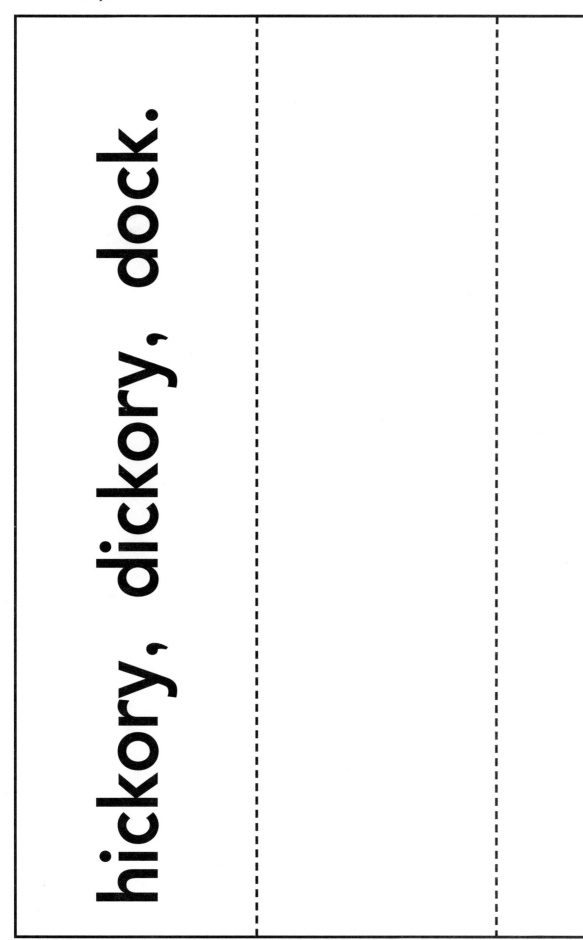

hickory, dickory, dock.

# Hickory, Dickory, Dock

# Hickory, Dickory, Dock

# Hickory, Dickory, Dock

# Hickory, Dickory, Dock

mouse

clock

up

down

one

148

# Mary Had a Little Lamb

Mary had a little lamb,

its fleece was white as snow.

And everywhere that Mary went,

the lamb was sure to go.

It followed her to school one day,

it was against the rule.

It made the students
laugh and play,

to see a lamb at school.

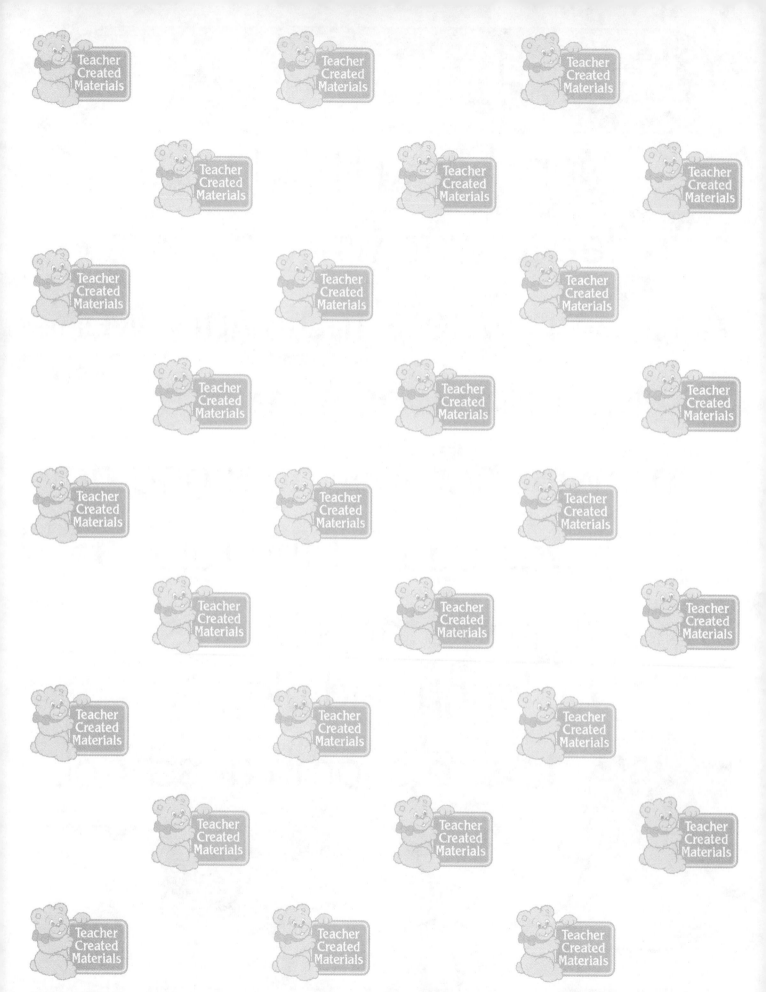

# Mary Had a Little Lamb

## Literacy Skills Activities

**Phonemic Awareness**—Have fun manipulating the first phoneme of the main words in each line. First, model for students deleting the first phoneme and reading the line *–ary –ad –a –ittle –amb.* Next, have an individual student choose a letter and reread the rhyme. For example, choose the phoneme, **b**—*Bary bad a bittle bamb.* To extend the activity, use small strips of paper to cover the initial letter(s) on the sentence strips. Write the replacement letter(s) on the strips of paper.

**Phonics**—Explain to the students that some words are not spelled the way they sound (phonetically). Find words in the rhyme that are not spelled the way they sound (*laugh, lamb*).
Have students say the letters the way they sound; then practice writing them correctly.

**Vocabulary Development**—What is *fleece?* Fleece is the wool that covers a lamb's body. Ask students to name things that are made from lamb's wool (*rugs, sweaters, seat covers, etc.*). Share a non-fiction book on the process of gathering wool from a lamb to create garments, etc.

**Fluency**—Read the rhyme very slowly, word by word, with no intonation. Then, read the rhyme fluently. Ask the students to determine which reading was more interesting and why.

**Comprehension Skills**—Instruct each student to choose a line from the rhyme and illustrate it. Then, have him or her write the line underneath the picture.

## Cross-Curricular Activities

**Social Studies**—Mary had a pet lamb. Ask students, "What pets do you have?" As a class, make a graph of the students' pets.

Mary's lamb broke the rule. Ask students, "What are some of the rules we have at school? Why are rules important?" Brainstorm with the students rules for the classroom.

**Math**—Make additional copies of the lamb pattern on page 155. Instruct students to create math problems using the lambs for manipulatives. Or, write a math problem on each lamb and place the answer on the back.

**Science**—Ask students, "What is a lamb?" (*A lamb is a baby sheep.*) With the students' help, make a list of other adult/baby animal names (*turkey/poult, cat/kitten, goose/gosling, elephant/calf, kangaroo/joey, cow/calf*). Extend the activity and have students name the adult male and adult female for each animal. (*For instance, a ram is a male sheep and a ewe is a female sheep.*)

Encourage students to collect and display wool samples, and things made from wool (*yarn, sweater, blanket, scarf, etc.*).

**Movement/Drama**—Allow students to play Animal Follow the Leader. Have them take turns being the leader. Suggest that the students choose different animals to portray while leading the group. First, suggest farm animals. Later, try ocean creatures, animals in the jungle, desert animals, etc.

# The Path to School

**Directions:** Help the lamb find Mary at school. Trace the path the lamb should take to find Mary.

# Mary Had a Little Lamb

## Materials

- file folder
- ruler
- scissors
- glue
- ⅛" hole punch
- 16"–18" (42 cm–46 cm) string
- clear tape
- tagboard
- patterns on pages 155–161 and copy of mini poster (page 149)

## Construction

1. Glue a copy of the nursery rhyme mini poster to the back of the file folder. Label the folder tab.

2. Cut out the schoolhouse and glue it to the inside of the folder in the upper left corner.

3. Cut out the left and right sides of the path.

4. Glue the smallest end of the path ⓐ on the folder below the door of the schoolhouse.

5. Glue the right side of the path ⓑ to the bottom of the right side of the folder. Make certain the paths meet at the crease of the folder.

6. Cut out the tree. Glue it to the folder above the path on the right side.

7. Cut out the flowers and place them around the tree and along the path.

8. Place one bird near the schoolhouse and one bird on the treetop.

9. Laminate the folder.

10. Cut out Mary and the lamb. For durability, glue each pattern to tagboard and cut them out.

11. Laminate Mary and the lamb.

12. Using the hole punch, punch 2 holes in the lamb (as shown) and 2 holes in the middle of Mary. Use the dots on the pattern as guides.

# Mary Had a Little Lamb

## Construction *(cont.)*

13. Punch a hole in the folder on the path below the schoolhouse.  Punch another hole on the lower right corner of the folder.

14. Insert the string through the holes in Mary and the lamb, making sure that Mary is between the lamb and the schoolhouse.  (Mary should be to the left of the lamb.)

15. Put the end of the string closest to Mary into the hole below the schoolhouse door and secure it on the back of the folder with clear tape.

16. Put the end of the string closest to the lamb into the hole at the end of the path and secure it on the back of the folder with clear tape.

17. Once Mary and the lamb are attached to the folder, make certain they can move back and forth easily.  If the two patterns do not move easily, remove the string and try again.

# Mary Had a Little Lamb

**Action Folder Patterns**

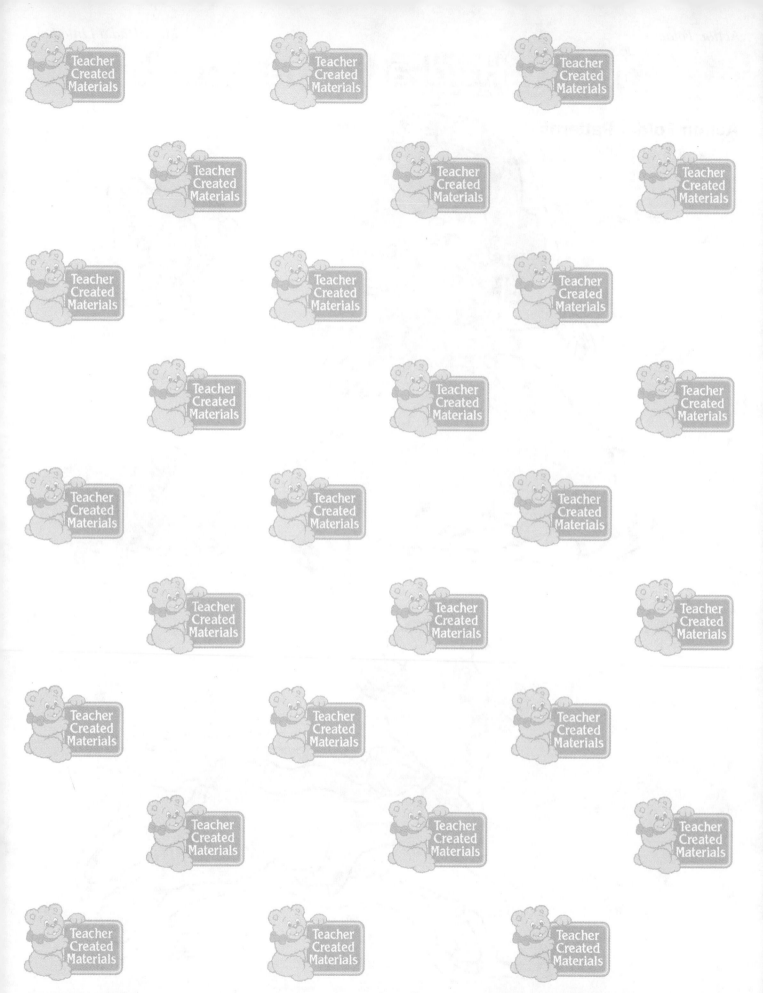

156

# Mary Had a Little Lamb

## Action Folder Patterns

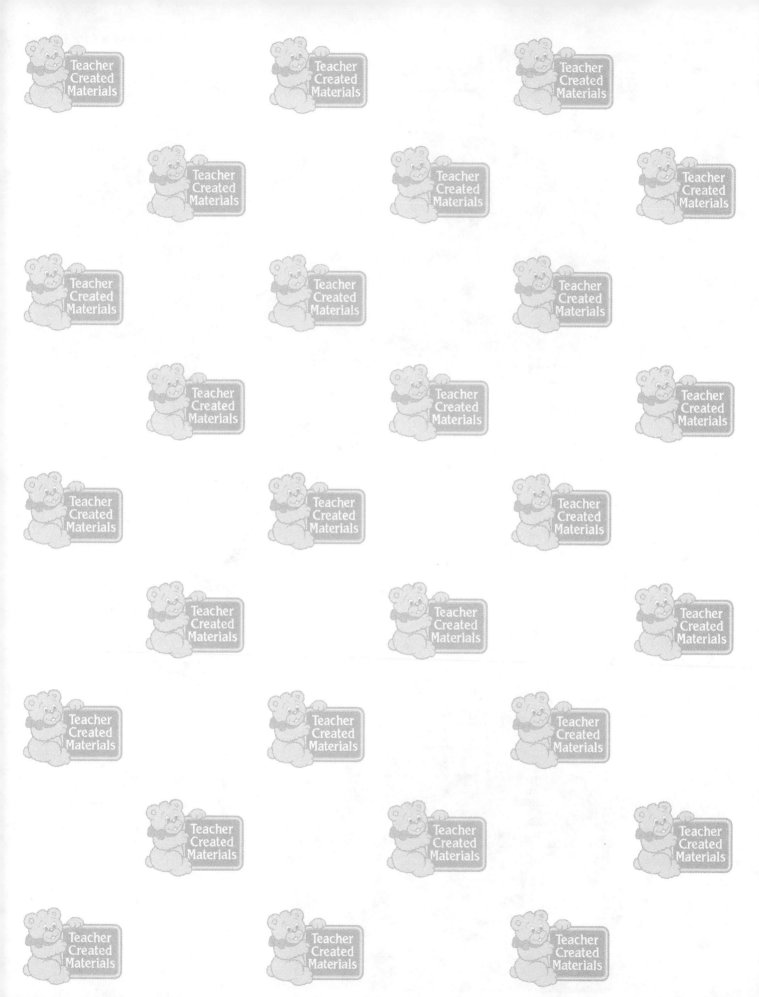

# Mary Had a Little Lamb

## Action Folder Patterns

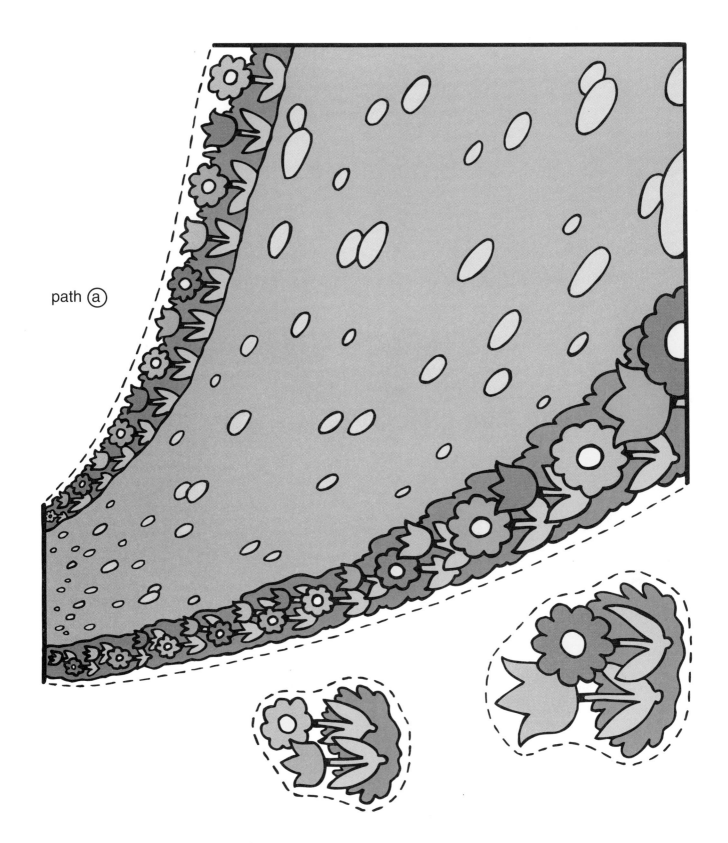

path (a)

160

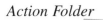

# Mary Had a Little Lamb

## Action Folder Patterns

path ⓑ

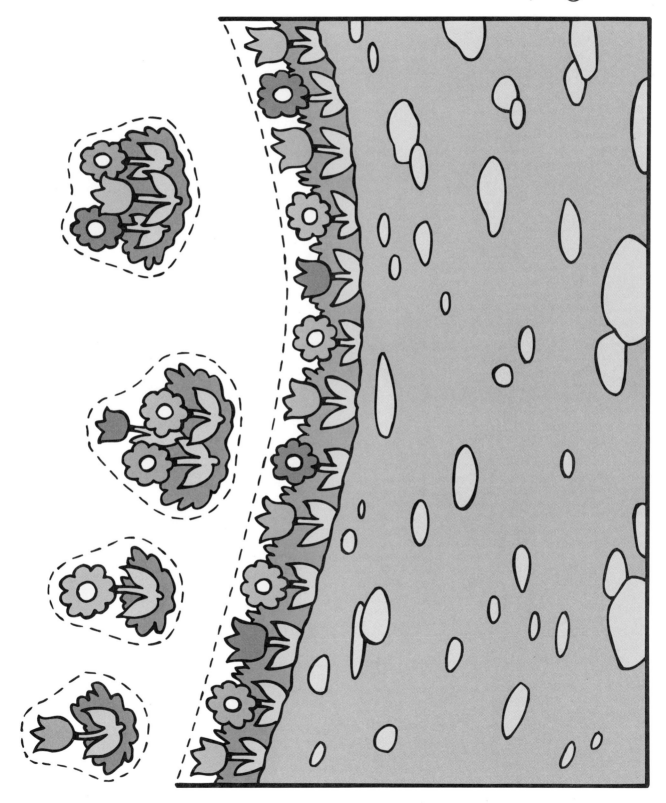

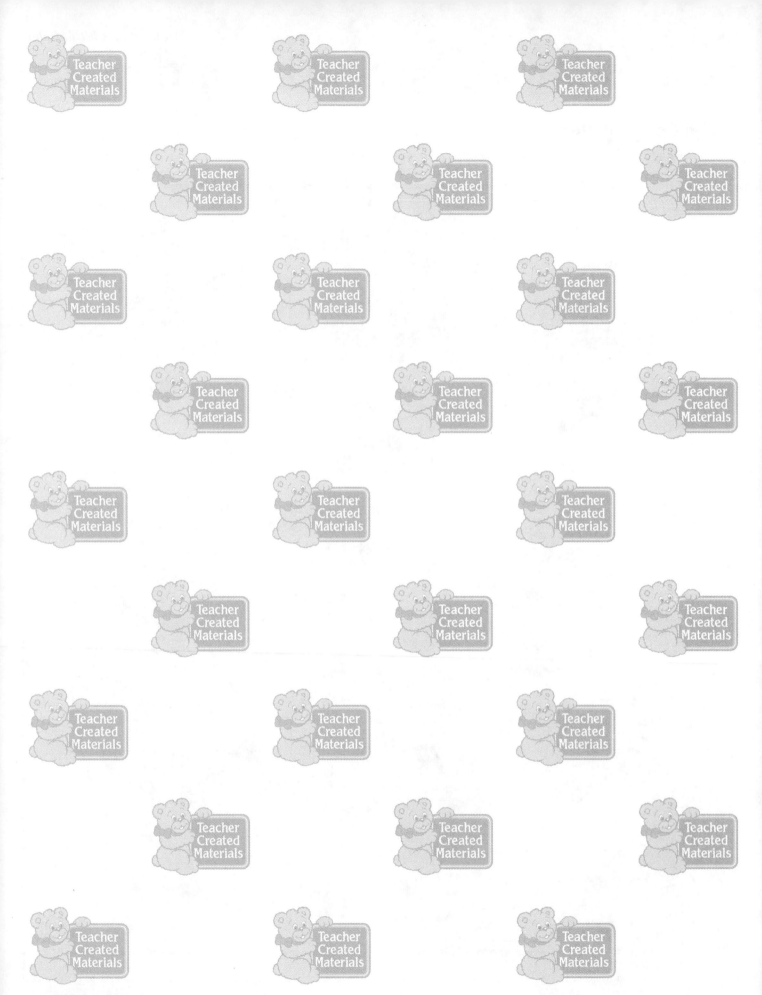

162

# Mary Had a Little Lamb

Mary had a little lamb,

its fleece was white as snow.

1

And everywhere that Mary went,

the lamb was sure to go.

**2**

It followed her to school one day,

it was against the rule.

**3**

It made the students laugh and play, **4**

to see a lamb at school. **5**

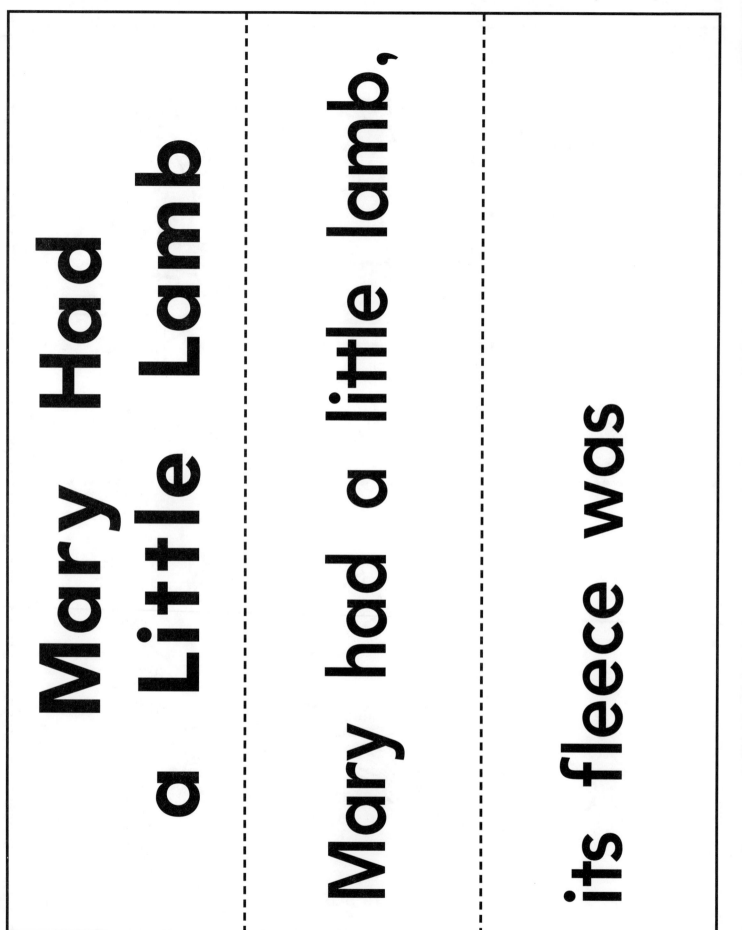

**Mary Had a Little Lamb**

**Mary had a little lamb,**

**its fleece was**

white as snow.

And everywhere

that Mary went,

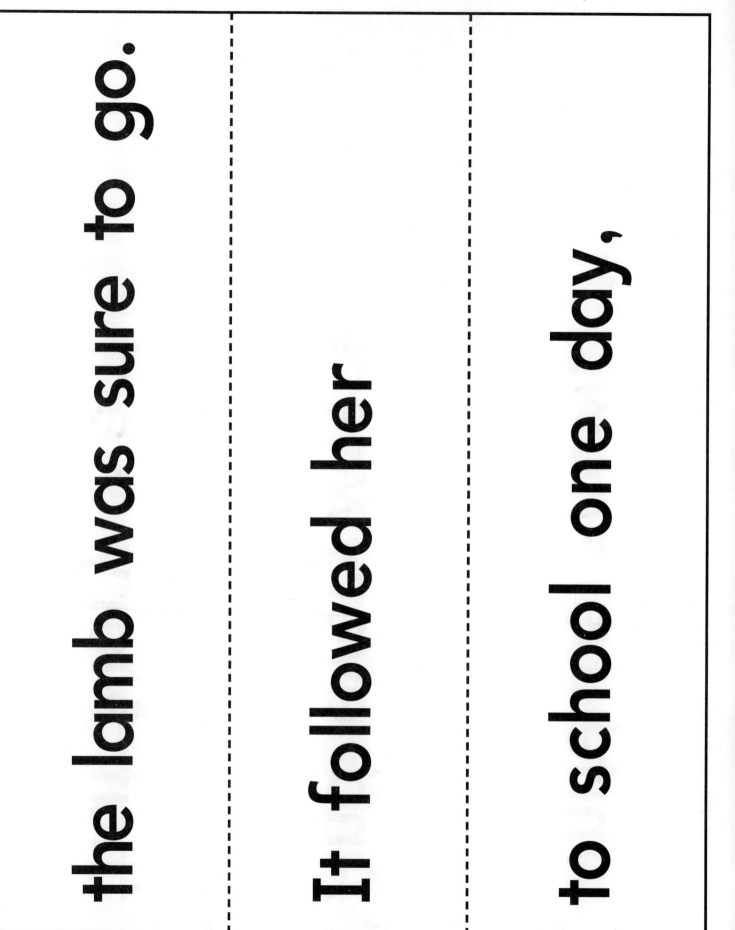

the lamb was sure to go.

It followed her

to school one day,

it was against

the rule.

It made the students

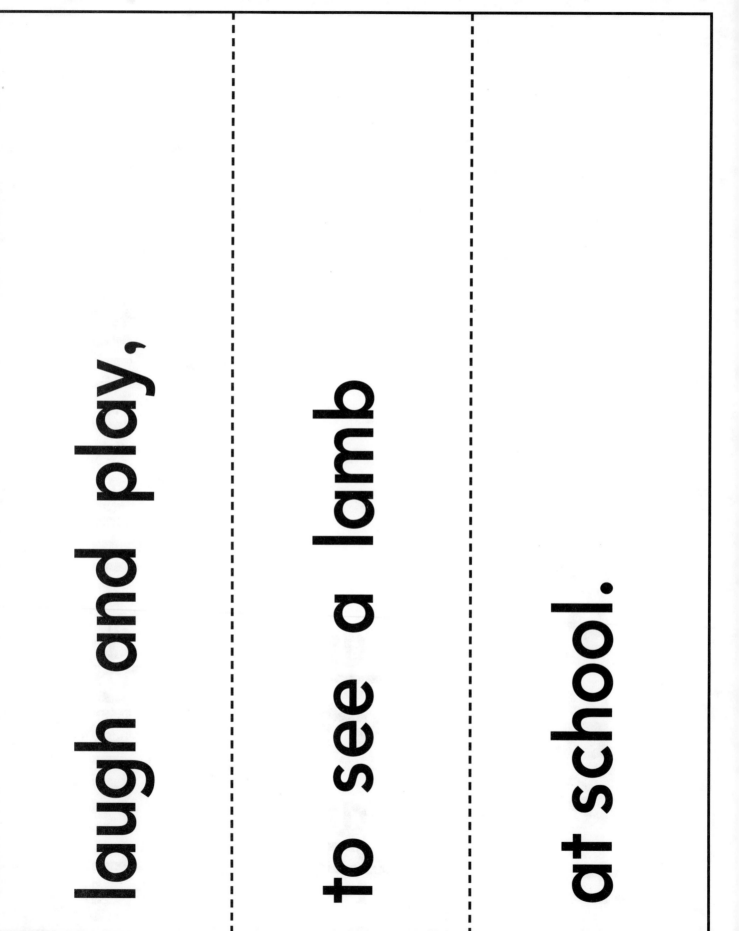

laugh and play,

to see a lamb

at school.

# Lamb Art Project

**Directions:** Glue cotton balls on the lamb. Cut out the lamb. Draw a picture of a pet that you would like to have in the box below.

My Favorite Pet

# Mary Had a Little Lamb

# Mary Had a Little Lamb

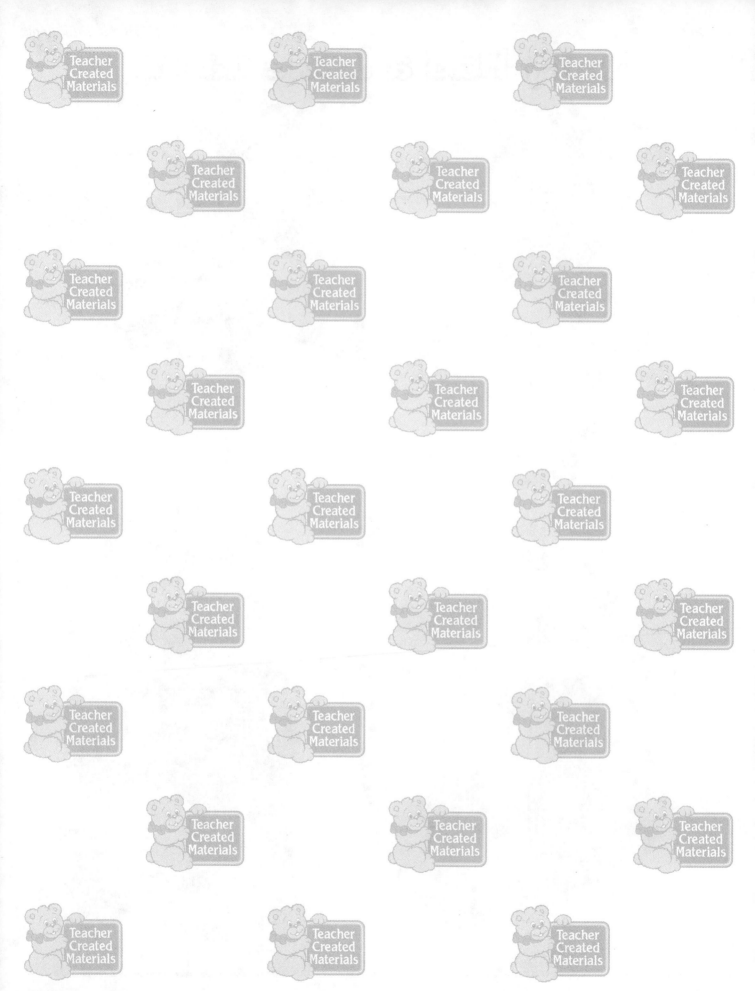

# Mary Had a Little Lamb

# Mary Had a Little Lamb

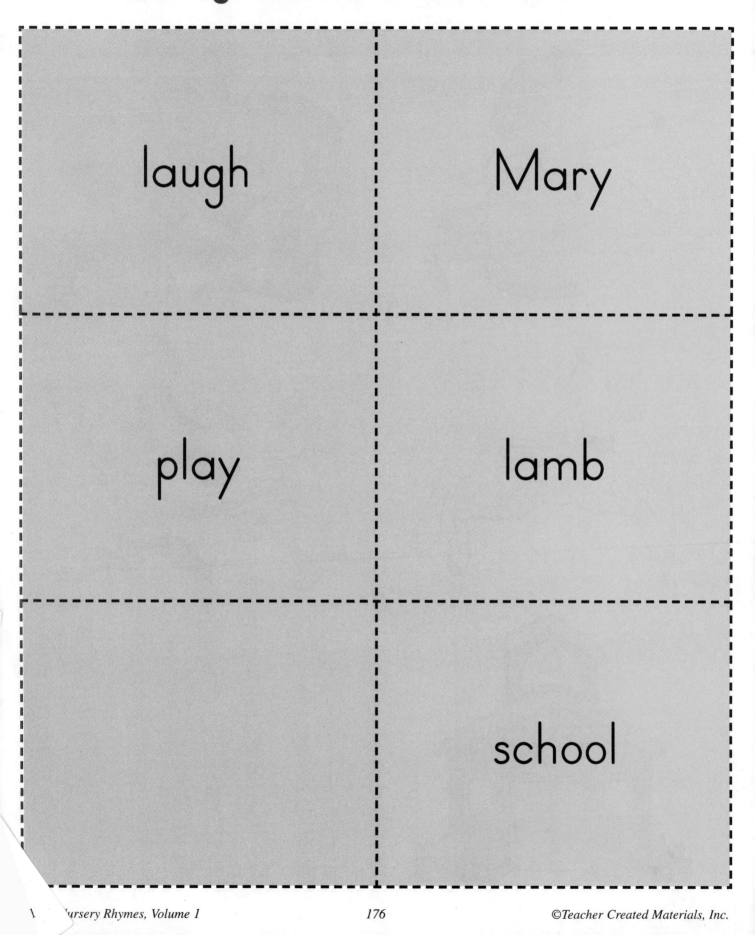

laugh

Mary

play

lamb

school